The Art of SHAPERSHIP™

The Art of SHAPERSHIP™

The Eye Only Sees What the Brain Is Ready to Understand

ALINE FRANKFORT and **JEAN-LOUIS BAUDOIN**

The Art of Shapership™
The Eye Only Sees What the Brain Is Ready to Understand

Copyright © 2023 by Aline Frankfort and Jean-Louis Baudoin

Shapership™ Publishing

All rights reserved solely by the author. The author guarantees all contents are original and do not infringe upon the legal rights of any other person or work. No part of this book may be reproduced in any form without the permission of the author.

ISBN-13: 979-8-218-14709-9

Library of Congress Control Number: 2023902592

To Edward de Bono

A genius, one of the funniest and kindest man on Earth, who, despite his brilliant and vanguard insights about the functioning of the Brain which gave birth to Lateral Thinking, and despite his considerable work and 80+ books on Efficient and Creative Thinking, did not succeed in eliminating useless Stupidity, but did indeed shape many people's Minds, from all ages, origins, genders, education levels and activities.

Your heritage is in our Minds, Hearts and Souls.

Table of Contents

Chapter 1
Introducing Shapership™ 1

Chapter 2
From "Nostalgia of the Future"
to the "Erotica of the Future" 15

Chapter 3
Who are the Shapers? 53

Chapter 4
The DNA of Shapership™ 63

Chapter 5
The "Do's and "Don'ts" of Shapership™:
from MAD land to NO MAD land 87

Chapter 6
Shapership put in action by some impressive People 133

Chapter 7
Some emerging and potential Shapers 209

Chapter 8
Shapership™ as a practice. 241

Chapter 9
What can Shapership™ bring
to organizations and Businesses? 265

Conclusions
To shape or not? To shape, that is the question! 283
About the Authors 287
Annex 293

Chapter 1
Introducing Shapership™

What's in a word?

As Friedrich Nietzsche, German philosopher and cultural critic said, *"Each word is a prejudice"*.

It opens or closes windows in our mind.

It is all about perceptions, not "truths".

What we propose here is a new concept which, we hope, will open new windows in your mind.

The word Shapership™ associates

- "Shaping" (as in "shaping a diamond")
- and "Ship" (meaning "a skill", as "craftsmanship" meaning a skill in a particular craft)

Shapership™ is the Art of shaping the Future.

It is the Art of making alternative and meaningful Futures visible and actionable.

THE ART OF SHAPERSHIP

It is the Art of shaping new Realities, opening up new paths to the Future and transforming Society for the better.

It means facing Reality in fresh, creative, visionary and sometimes revolutionary ways, with a clear acknowledgment of *"what is"* and a Transformative Vision of *"what could be"*, associated with perfectly connected and aligned transformative actions.

Above all, Shapership™ is a way to be and to "look" at the world, being completely aware that *"the eye only sees what the brain is ready to understand"* [1].

It is a fundamental attitude and aptitude to "see" what is possible, beyond "what is", and certainly beyond what is commonly accepted as "possible" by a majority.

Shapership™ stands for "more Imagination and more Freedom to make radically different and meaningful Futures emerge, in tune with the highest human Hopes and aspirations.

Why this new concept?

Because this is what the world needs: new shapes, new forms, new perspectives and new approaches.

1. Our Planet, our world, our societies and our organisations are dying of our rigid, mechanical and Imagination-less thinking approaches. Business as Usual must stop! So does the "Thinking as Usual" that generates it!

   Our lack of Imagination and of new "meaning-making" stories – our inability to imagine a Future that is different from the Present - are catastrophic! They lead to Fear, Despair, Cynicism, even to Violence

---

[1] Henri Bergson, French Philosopher, The Creative Mind: An Introduction to Metaphysics (Dover Publications Inc, 2010), 175

and to the endless Repetition of the S.O.S - Same Old Solutions (short-term) - which pretend to solve problems using the same old obsolete paradigm. The kind of attitude that leads the ostrich to bury its head in the sand!

2. "We are living not in an era of Change, but in a change of Era".[2] It is obvious that we will not be able to solve 21st century issues with 19th and 20th centuries ways of thinking and acting. What is needed is a **shift in perspectives**. The huge amount of changes in the "macrocosm" calls for enormous changes in the "microcosm" – the one between our ears. It is useless and risky to respond to new situations with old perspectives

3. **We need to make a wise move: from MAD Land to NO-MAD Land.** It is a secret for no one that our current world is going **M.A.D.** More exactly, the way we live on this planet is leading us to *Mutually Assured Destruction.* [3]It is easy to feel overwhelmed and depressed by this situation. What we propose is something else: a place of Hope, Wisdom, Imagination and Desire to build a **NO-MAD** World based on no Madness

4. Without Imagination, we are stuck in the dominant worldviews of Neoliberalism (a political approach that favors free-market capitalism, deregulation, and reduction in government spending): the story of Scarcity, Separation, Competition, Efficiency, Infinite Growth, Power over others, etc. We need an alternative story of the Future that resonates with our deepest Aspirations and provides an actionable

---

[2] Jan Rotmans, professor of transition studies and sustainability

[3] Mutual Assured Destruction, or Mutually Assured Destruction (MAD) is a doctrine of military strategy and national security policy in which a full-scale use of high-yield weapons by two opposing sides would effectively result in the complete, utter and irrevocable annihilation of both the attacker and the defender

guide to a viable Human Future. A narrative able to generate an **"erotic" attraction for the Future**.

Without that new story, Hope vanishes, Fear, Despair, Fatalism, and Cynicism supersede the desire to move forward

5. We cannot wait for some "enlightened" leaders to make those changes.

"Deep down though, we know that when we turn to our Leaders for solutions, we are looking in the wrong place, in the wrong way. "[4]

We have reached a time when many people "at the top" want to retain Power although they cruelly lack the needed "Authority", the inspiring Vision, the Wisdom and the Awareness. For many reasons, these people tackle an **Eco-System Reality** with an **Ego-System Perspective.**

6. Many people - and among them some really young ones - aspire to change the world in radical and transformative ways. They know our ways of Life – and our ways to destroy Life – must make place for other approaches to See, Think and Act instead of keeping conforming to obsolete models. They resist the dominant worldviews of the MAD world. In their heart, they feel an aspiration to live a meaningful Life and to make a difference rather than to make a career. Some of them are already creating alternative Futures that include their dreams and aspirations. While many others are locked in Confusion, Hopelessness, Desperation or Cynicism. They know the Life they don't want but don't find the force and imagination to create the one they want. Shapership™ can help them change their perceptions, boost their Imagination to

---

[4] Collective Presencing: A New Human Capacity. By Ria Baeck and Helen Titchen Beeth. Kosmos, Spring | Summer2012 = http://www.kosmos-journal.org/articles/collective-presencing-a-new-human-capacity

create alternative "stories" and shape their Lives in meaningful, desirable, and hopeful ways.

7. Everywhere around the world, in the most famous universities – including corporate universities – courses on "Leadership" and "Entrepreneurship" proliferate, as if those were the only two solutions to "save the world". They definitely are not if they operate with old guard "lenses" and paradigms.

The inherited vocabulary around Leadership / Entrepreneurship and the "windows" it opens in our minds are no longer adapted to help us adequately face the complex challenges of our times. Shapership™ opens more appropriate perspectives.

The fact is, **in today's interconnected world,**

- You don't have to be a Leader or to have a "title" to do something meaningful and to make an impact
- You don't have to be someone "important" to take a stand and reshape things

Shapership™ is neither Leadership, nor Entrepreneurship, but connections exist, of course, and mutual enrichments can be achieved.

THE ART OF SHAPERSHIP

What is Shapership™ about?

Shapership™ is about aiming at imagining and transforming the world, in order to resist Stupidity, Fear, Despair and Violence.

It is infused with Courage, Hope, Imagination, Wisdom and Freedom which all reinforce each other in a virtuous circle.

Imagination opens new radically different and meaningful Futures, in tune with the highest human Hopes and Aspirations. It requires Freedom and gives Freedom of choice. It requires the type of Courage that allows to resist Fear, challenge dominant stories and it reinforces Courage.

That's why we say that Shapership™ stands for "more Imagination and more Freedom to foster Radical Wisdom and a strong Desire for Meaningful Futures"

Ultimately, it stands for building the Future on wise choices.

Because our wisest decisions are made from Desire and Hope rather than from Despair, Fear, or "Repetition", we focus on "Radical Imagination" as a force able to generate an "erotic attraction of the Future".

It is an attitude of Radical Authenticity, Creative Imagination and Unconventional Wisdom which leads to escape from the prison of our "representations", to see things with fresh eyes, to challenge the status quo, to unlock Imagination to generate Life-affirming transformative approaches, attitudes and behaviours that give us Hope that a viable Future is possible.

It is Thinking big and radically different about oneself and how we want to participate in the transformation of the world for ourselves, our communities and Society as a whole.

It is focused on discovering and making meaningful and desirable stories of the Future Visible and actionable.

It is about being an "I Opener", an "Eye Opener", an "Eye Hopener" and a "High Hopener". It is opening ourself, opening eyes which have new types of visions which generate Hope and help others elevate theirs.

The Shapership™ Attitude rises from the inner Consciousness and "*Soul Compass*" which "know"

1. that the "way things are" needs to be challenged": status quo must be resisted as well as our "routine Thinking". We call it the Big "NO": Creative Resistance.

2. that another and more beautiful "world" is possible, that "*what is possible is richer than what is.*" [5]

    That's what we call The Big "YES": The Transformative Vision, which opens new paths towards the Future.

3. that a transformative Vision calls for transformative actions and that it will require courage to completely reinvent the way things operate, to shift from one paradigm to another. That's what we call the "Creative How": Anticipative Experimentation.

This is in fact the DNA of Shapership™.

Shapership™ is an enlarged Perception or Vision.

It means adopting vanguard lenses and paradigm shifting visions, allowing for a creative reconstruction of what we commonly accept as THE "Reality".

It is about our capacity to change our "Reality".

This requires that we understand that we do indeed see the world through particular lenses and that we have the freedom and the power to change those lenses.

In other words, we create stories, and these stories shape our lives.

---

[5] Henri Bergson, French Philosopher

THE ART OF SHAPERSHIP

When we change those stories, we can change the way we shape our world.

This requires a Paradigm Shift: A Shift in Thinking and in Perspectives.

It means changing how we think and what we think.

The Shapership™ attitude offers a vehicle to move from a MAD world to a NO-MAD world. Not to correct the Past but to invent an alternative meaning-making-story based on completely different worldviews.

Instead of trying to "*solve*" current problems within the same paradigm, the aim is to "*dissolve*" them. The Shapership™ attitude is inspired by the great scientist Buckminster Fuller who said:

> "*You never change things by fighting the existing Reality. To change something, build a new model that makes the existing model obsolete*".

What we call "Shapership™" is this vital capacity to "shift" perspectives and "craft" Reality: The Art of Shaping the Future.

Insert 1: The Metaphor of Pottery

> *One metaphor might help to describe the "Art" of Shaping the Future: The Art of Pottery.*
>
> *The potter transforms a lump of clay into a beautiful Shape, thanks to a deep knowledge of his Art, an intimacy with the material at hand, working at the same time with a Vision in his Mind and his hands "in the Matter". The whole process of Thinking and Acting are parts of a fluid and real-time process*

of Interaction and Creation which leaves room for unforeseen aspects, Intuition and Inspiration. [6]

Similarly, Shapership™ is a way to craft Reality with a full connection between "Head, Heart and Hands". In other words, Alignment between

- *Vision and Action (experimentation)*
- *Abstract and concrete levels*
- *Helicopter view and concrete Knowledge of the "material" at hand.*
- *Open Mind, Open Heart, Open Will* [7] *which less politely said is "Brain, Heart and Guts"*
- *The Why? (Intention), the How? (Process) and the What? (Action)*
- *The Self and Life, in line with the saying "Life is what happens to us while we are busy making other plans", demanding that we give up control and opt for intuition driven by Knowledge and Inspiration*

What you will find in this book

In the following pages, we introduce an approach that can be an inspiration to anyone – regardless of origin, gender, colour, country, educational level, status, domain of expertise, social group or Culture, - to become a Shaper of

---

[6] As a permanent inspiration, we are very grateful to Henry Mintzberg for his work and in particular for his enlightening Article, "Crafting Strategy", Harvard Business Review, 1987

[7] We borrow this concept from Otto Sharmer's "Theory U", with whom we attended an executive training on "Transformational Leadership » at the Sloan Management School (MIT) in 2003

THE ART OF SHAPERSHIP

the Future or to add certain dimensions of Shapership™ to one's current existence.

The book is divided into nine Chapters.

The next Chapter, *"From Nostalgia to Erotica of the Future"* provides background on the way we, Humans, make sense of Reality through stories. It gives a perspective on how these "representations" create our experience of Reality and impact our ability or inability to imagine a Future which is different than the Present. We propose "Radical Imagination" as a force able to generate an "Erotic attraction to the Future" and help us make wise decisions today, based on Desire and Hope rather than on Despair, Fear, or "Repetition".

Chapter three, *"Who are the Shapers"*, provides a poetic description and a non-exhaustive list of the people who, from our point of view, embody the concept. We call them *"Shapers"*. They have "changed the world", at least part of it. They have opened new paths - in Education, Justice, Management, Health, just to name a few. - which were invisible until they came along.

Shapers have been around as long as we can remember! They appear in every country, social groups, fields of activity, age-brackets, genders, races and contexts.

We focused on the way Shapers perceive the world, i.e. on their way of seeing, being and acting to make alternative and meaningful Futures visible and actionable.

All of them have one thing in common: they think "big" and creative.

All of them practice what we describe in Chapter four, "The DNA of Shapership™".

What we discovered is very simple and the short summary here might enlighten the reading of the first chapters of the book.

As a way of being, Shapership™ invites to adopt the "Altitude Attitude" and to open the "Soul Compass". It is an integrity of the Being based on a full connection between Open Mind, Open Heart and Open Will.

It gives Shapers the capacity to see / think Big and Radical, to adopt a helicopter view yet in tune with Reality, to act from a deeply connected perspective, way beyond Ego awareness, and to open meaningful and progress-generating trails for the entire human "Eco-system".

As a way of doing, Shapership™ derives its power from the articulation of three very simple elements that all Shapers activate, as anyone can do in his/her everyday life. To indicate *Radicality (going to the roots)*, we have qualified them as follows

1. **Creative Resistance: The Big "NO".**

    While most people accept a given situation as "just the way things are", Shapers perceive the status quo as something to be overcome or disrupted. Creative Resistance emerges from looking at Reality square in the face and sensing the need for something else to be born.

    By looking at reality in a fresh way, Shapers initiate a creative reconstruction of what is possible. They challenge orthodox approaches and the S.O.S. (Same Old Solutions) that only serves to preserve the Past or "fix" the problem within the same paradigm, which they know is unsustainable in the long-term

    While Creative Resistance is a durable attitude, it is not enough on its own. It leads to a desire to move forward and shape the Future through Creative Transformations. Shapers take a stand!

2. The Transformative Vision: The Big "YES".

Shapers embrace "what could be" and set out to bring it to life, reinforced by a deep commitment to a meaningful and Transformative Vision which is making alternative Futures visible. It is Martin Luther King's "I have a Dream", which opens the hearts of millions of people. It is a big "YES" to a desired Future, something that "needs to happen" because it represents the Hopes of many and enhances the Dignity and the meaning of human Life.

So, even if others think it is "impossible", Shapers fully engage and make the impossible possible!

Using this vision as a "lens", Shapers open up new paths towards the Future, embodying the change they want to see happen in the world.

As they go about practicing what they preach, their transformative vision becomes the axis upon which they align their thoughts and actions.

3. Anticipative Experimentation: The Creative "HOW"

To begin to shape new realities in an alternative Paradigm, Shapers often need to completely reinvent the ways things operate. They know key issues require system solutions.

To achieve this, they abolish Competition and create new forms of Collaboration.

They rally a dynamic ecosystem of actors and partners, so that Anticipative Experimentation becomes a space for co-creation. Whether it is through a movement, a company, a community, Shapers unite people around shared Purposes and make the transition path visible.

Chapter five, "The Do's and Don'ts" of Shapership™ introduces a possibility to Shift from MAD Land, our current world based on Massive Assured Destruction to NO MAD Land. It uses the metamorphosis of the voracious Caterpillar into the Butterfly, the animal with the lightest touch on earth as a powerful metaphor of the current situation and the choices we have.

Chapter six, "Shapership™ put in Action by some famous Shapers" contains the stories of the people we chose as examples and an inspiration, all over the world. Some are dead, some alive, the youngest was fifteen.

Chapter seven is dedicated to "Some emerging and potential Shapers", the youngest being aged fifteen at the time of his emergence. Considering his fame, we decided to put on our Shapership™ lenses to look at "The case of Elon Musk" and raise the question: is he a Shaper?

Chapter eight, "Shapership™ as a practice" offers new insights and examples of applications, not as a toolbox per see but as sources of pragmatic inspiration and reflective surfaces.

Chapter nine addresses a specific question: "What can Shapership™ mean and bring to organisations and Businesses?

Shapership™ may be adopted by any persons or "communities of work" who aspire to put their Courage, Soul, Wisdom, Imagination, Creativity and Passion at work to open new paths to the Future and drive pioneering Wealth-Creation (intellectual, cultural, social, emotional, economic) in an "alternative" paradigm, based on radically different values and worldviews that can lead Humanity to become more humane.

Chapter 2

From "Nostalgia of the Future" to the "Erotica of the Future"

As Jason Fried & David Heinemeier Hansson, brilliantly put it in their book "Rework" [8]: *"The real world isn't a place, it's an excuse. It's a justification for not trying"*.

We all recall moments in our life when we were talking about our "wildest dreams" for our Future and heard the famous sentence "it is impossible", "it won't work", "it is not realistic"... or even, "you are an idealist".

As so called "adults", what happened to our "impossible dreams" and hopes? Are we using "Reality as an excuse"?

The point is that, especially in these turbulent times, it is very difficult to make sense of the "real world".

Our friend Graham Leicester – Director of International Futures Forum points out very precisely:

> *"We live in the age of the missing elephant". (...)
> The world we have created has outstripped*

---

[8] Rework, Jason Fried & David Heinemeir Hansson, Crow Business, ISBN 978-0-307-46374-6

> *our capacity to understand it. The scale of interconnectivity and interdependence has resulted in a step change in the complexity of the operating environment. These new conditions are raising fundamental questions about our competence in key areas of governance, economy, sustainability and consciousness. We are struggling as professionals and in our private lives to meet the demands they are placing on traditional models of organisations, understanding and action. The anchors of identity, morality, cultural coherence and social stability are unravelling, and we are losing our bearings; this is a conceptual emergency."[9]*

We (Aline and Jean-Louis) don't pretend to bring "explanations" about the state of the world. Nor to decode what is happening outside and even less to predict what could happen.

Our wish is, in the simplest possible manner, to enrich the understanding of the way we, Humans, look at "Reality", form perceptions, make sense of the world through stories and make decisions that will, in turn, shape our Reality, i.e. our experience of Life.

In other words, depending on the way we perceive Reality "as it is" and "as it could be", we have the choice to move from a "Nostalgia" to an "Erotica of the Future": a passionate desire for the Future.

By consciously being aware and choosing the way we look at "Reality", by adopting the Altitude Attitude, by shifting our perspectives, we can form new perceptions. We can make wiser choices and live a life full of possibilities.

---

[9] Ten Things to do in a conceptual Emergency, Graham Leicester & Maureen O'Hara, International Futures Forum

This is called the "Art of Re-perception": changing our maps so we can change the Landscape.

Our hope is that it will allow to build the Future on wise decisions.

"We cannot predict the Future, but we can co-create a healthier Future through appropriate design decisions informed by the integral Wisdom of multiple Perspectives."[10]

Reality as a "Meaning-Making Story"

Most words which end up in "ity" – such as Reality, Productivity, Creativity, Plausibility, Fraternity, Egality- indicate a relationship.

For instance,

- Productivity is the relationship between Production capacity and constraints
- Creativity is Value creation within well-defined constraints (think of an architect who must be as creative as possible within the limits of his client's needs, available space, time, budgets, amongst others.)
- Plausibility is the relationship between what is plausible (what might happen) and our perceptions (what we believe at a given moment).

We all know that despite all our conceptual and technical efforts, we, humans, don't have access to the "Real as it is". We only have access to our own "representations".

---

[10] Daniel Christian Wahl, https://medium.com/age-of-awareness/co-designing-our-future-8557caa3a448

THE ART OF SHAPERSHIP

Insert 2: We create our own Reality

Reality
= a more or less creative reconstruction
= a meaning making story

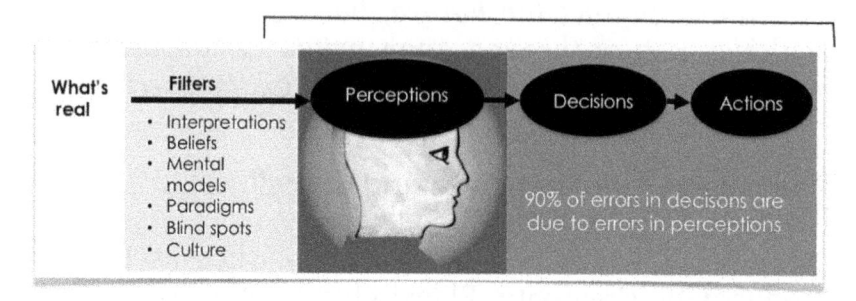

What's real	Filters			
	• Interpretations • Beliefs • Mental models • Paradigms • Blind spots • Culture	Perceptions →	Decisions →	Actions

90% of errors in decisons are due to errors in perceptions

What we call Reality is the "real" (what exists) within the limits of our perceptions. It is a "creative" reconstruction of the "real", filtered by our interpretations, lenses, paradigms and mental models.

Perceptions are stories we tell ourselves.

And stories we believe.

David Bohm, one of the most significant theoretical physicists of the 20th century [11], called perceptions "Theories of the Mind" to clearly indicate that they are our hypothesis and should be considered as such.

We each have our own Reality. At the individual and collective level, Reality is a creation, a more or less creative reconstruction of "what is" which is often confused with "Truth".

For instance, we all have our own interpretation of the words "Happiness", "Success", "Brotherhood", "Family", "Transmission", "Mastery", "Art", "Performance", "Respect", "Authority" ...and all those words are likely to take on very different meanings in different cultures and at different times.

---

[11] David Bohm, "Wholeness and the Implicate Order", 1980

"What's in a word? A world"[12]

Let's add, what's in a comma?

You have probably all heard this question that Hamlet asks himself as he contemplates a skull: *"To be or not to be, that is the question."*

Linguists have hypothesized that the copyist made a mistake in the placement of the comma and that the closest version of what Shakespeare meant was in reality: *"To be or not. To be, that is the question."*

A whole different story.

This is true even when words are replaced by numbers

Just for the fun of it, look at the following operation:

$$3 + 3 \times 3 + 3$$

It can be answered 3 different ways, and everybody is right: 15, 21, 36

$$3 + (3 \times 3) + 3 = 15$$
$$(3 + 3) \times 3 + 3 = 21$$
$$(3 + 3) \times (3 + 3) = 36$$

Everything is a question of how we look at a situation.

Just as we design buildings that end up shaping our lives, we create stories that shape our Lives.

Arthur Frank tells us: *"Once stories are under people's skin, they affect the terms in which people think, know, and perceive"*. [13]

---

[12] Narrative means to therapeutic ends, Michael White & David Epston

[13] Arthur Frank, *Letting stories breathe: a socio-narratology*. Chicago: The University of Chigaco Press, 2012, page 48

THE ART OF SHAPERSHIP

We do not live by consciously telling ourselves that we are telling ourselves a story.

Stories are felt to be lifelike: indeed, they are felt as Life itself.

Our stories "write" our lives. They shape our sense of Identity, what we believe as "true" and "possible" at a given moment of our life (or forever if we are very rigid), our Future, the meaning we give to our experiences, the decisions we make.

Stories are the way we make sense of our Lives.

We call them the "*Meaning-Making Story*" of who we are and of what the world is.

It is through these stories that we tell ourselves the Past, The Present and even the Future.

Indeed, what is Life but a "Meaning-Making Story"?

What is a Religion but a "Meaning-Making Story"?

What is a Utopia but a "Meaning-Making Story" of the Future?

What is a Corporate Vision or a Strategy but a "Meaning-Making Story" of the Future for that specific Community?

Even a white page can be a "Meaning-Making Story".

> *In a Buddhist temple, a monk is crying.*
>
> *One of the brothers approaches him and asks, "What is happening to you?»*
>
> *The first answers: look at this, what do you see?*
>
> *He shows his brother a white page with a red dot.*
>
> *The second one says: a red stain*
>
> *The first one starts crying again and says: that's exactly what makes me sad. I have been showing this to all our brothers for a week*

now, asking them what they see, and they all answer me like you do; "a red stain". Not one of them answered "a blank page".

The fact is that Perceptions are a sort of *"Theatre of our Mind"* and this "representation" creates our experience of reality and the way we make sense of it! We could almost say that "Life is a Theatre".

Here is a wonderful story to illustrate this.

> *One day in 1924, Niels Bohr and Werner Heisenberg, two great Physicists, are having a conversation in Kronberg Castle in Denmark. The castle where legend tells us Hamlet lived.*
> *At one point, Niels Bohr tells his friend: "Isn't it strange how this castle instantly changes as soon as we imagine Hamlet lived here! As scientists, we believe a castle is essentially made of stones and we admire the way the architect has conceived the whole. And all this shouldn't be modified by the fact that Hamlet lived here, and yet, it changes everything. Suddenly, the ramparts and the walls speak another language, the courtyard becomes another world, a dark corner reflects the human soul and we hear Hamlet say "To be or not? To be, that is the question!"*[14]

When Maps change the Landscape

It is not about the things we look at. It is about the way we look at things.

---

[14] Keith H. Basso, Wisdom sits in places: Landscape and Language among the Western Apache, (University of New Mexico Press, 1996), 5-6

THE ART OF SHAPERSHIP

We assume that "outside" circumstances shape our stories. But it is the exact opposite which happens: the stories we tell have the power to shape our lives.

"Vision" creates Reality. **The way we look at things changes our Lives.**

And, as the story above demonstrates, what we "imagine" transforms our experience of Reality.

The key point is that our "mental" maps are not the "landscape", but they define how we shape the landscape.

But what happens when the stories we tell are misleading or incomplete or just wrong? They keep us "stuck".

Why is this crucial?

Because every day, we make decisions and act according to our perceptions, which are more or less accurate, open, imaginative and Future-relevant "stories"

> *"Studies have shown that 90% of errors in Thinking are due to errors in Perception. If you can change your Perceptions, you can change your emotions, and this can lead to new ideas."*[15]

Deciding is also imagining. It is being capable of envisaging the "non-impossible", of reaching the capacity to overcome the certainties and the uncertainties that we have. It is often an "exercise in ignorance" because there are more unknowns than knowns in the Future.

This raises two questions:

The first is: we are map makers but are we aware of our "mental Atlas? "

---

[15] Dr. Edward de Bono, Doctor in Psychology, Medicine and Philosophy. Author of more than 80 books and one of the world's highest Authority on Serious Creativity

Alfred Korzybski, a Polish American Scholar said "the word dog doesn't bite"; he also said

> *"The map is not the territory"*[16]

Everyone understands that but, in depth, what kind of attention do we actually bring to the *"Theatre of our Minds"*, to this imaginary world we create, through which we interpret the world, and which guides our decisions, our actions and our lives?

The second is even more important: is it possible that we try to create the Future starting from obsolete maps? In other words, from imaginary worlds which lack Imagination?

Change the Story, Change the World

We (Aline and Jean-Louis) are driven by a conviction: when we change the stories that shape our lives, we can change the way we shape our lives and the world.

It is time to reverse the traditional way of looking at things, attributed to Saint Thomas:

> *"I only believe what I see"*.

By the way, we perfectly know it is mostly untrue: the majority of people don't see what they don't believe in. Or worse, some can't believe what they know: they prefer to give up facts which contradict their beliefs rather than change their beliefs.

Actually, taking into account the gap between knowing and believing, a more appropriate description of our "normal" approach could be: *"I see what I believe."*

---

[16] Alfred Korsybski, Science and Sanity. an introduction to Non-Aristotelian Systems and General Semantics (Ed. Institute of General Semantics, 5th ed, 2000), 747

What we propose here is the following: consciously open "eyes" which have new sort of Visions.

> **"The eye only sees what the brain is ready to understand".**[17]

This idea is at the core of Shapership™.

All ancient Wisdoms say it in their own way. One attributed to Buddha is

> "What you think, you become it. What you feel, you attract it. What you imagine, you create it".

Since 1925, Quantum physicists say what is now proven by Modern Physics: **"It is our mind that defines Reality and not the opposite"** [18]

This is scientific fact.

Vision creates Reality: Consciousness is creating our life experience of Reality.

And "Reality" is a story we tell ourselves which shapes our lives, sometimes by limiting our sense of possibilities.

Then, what if we change our Consciousness?

Then we change our Reality.

That's great because it is a lot easier to change the "microcosm between our ears" than to build a whole new world out there.

Changing our "Reality" starts with the simple awareness that we have the power to change the way we look at things.

It is not a question of "seeing to believe" but of "changing what we believe" – for instance thanks to knowledge

---

[17] Henri Bergson

[18] Among modern physicists, Philippe Guillemant - « la Route du temps », Ed. Guy Tredaniel, 2014 – and Thibault Damour

– and "believing to create". We need to make a crack in our "imaginary".

By changing our consciousness, a whole new reality will manifest itself.

What are we ready to understand?
What do we believe is true?
What do we believe is possible?

One of the main points about perceptions is that they define what we *believe* is possible or impossible for our lives and in life.

There are famous stories which demonstrate this.

For instance, do you remember Roger Bannister? He has been the first athlete to break the "impossible" four-minute mile running? Until he did, it was simply assumed that human beings could not run that fast. Physiologists and other "authorities" said that not only was running the four-minute mile impossible but that attempting it was even dangerous. What is interesting is that, in the years that followed, dozens of other athletes achieved the same performance. Why? Because Bannister's act shifted their belief about what was possible!

Another story about the "impossible possible is the one of Arthur Tatum Jr. (October 13, 1909 – November 5, 1956). He was an American Jazz pianist who is widely regarded as one of the greatest of all times.

From infancy, Tatum had impaired vision. Several explanations for this have been presented, most involving cataracts. He had eye operations, which meant that at the age of eleven, he could see things that were close to him, and perhaps could distinguish colours. Any benefits from these procedures were reversed, however, when he was assaulted, probably in his early twenties, which left him completely blind in his left eye and with very limited vision in his right.

THE ART OF SHAPERSHIP

He began playing the piano by ear from a young age, aided by an excellent memory and sense of pitch (some say a perfect sense of pitch).

The legend says that his playing style developed because he was able to reproduce piano roll recordings made by two pianists playing together. And that is exactly what his playing lead to believe: that he played as if he had four hands.

In other words, he did not know it was impossible. So, he did it.

Human beings probably did not change much since the Philosopher Seneca pointed out at the beginning of our era: *"It's not because things are difficult that we don't dare to do them, it's because we don't dare that they are difficult."*

In some cases, our Reality is our own "prison"

There is nothing new to that.

Remember Plato's famous "Allegory of the Cave"!

Imprisoned men are chained in a cave and can only see the shadows of objects moved by puppeteers and projected on the wall in front of them. Those men confuse the "shadows" with the "real things".

We are like those men, imprisoned by what we BELIEVE is Reality, trapped in our representations of the world, in our habits, our prejudices, our usual and known answers.

If we don't know that "another world" is possible, we certainly believe that what we see is Reality.

But, in this Allegory, Plato tells us that, one day, a man is freed (he could also have heard an interior call and freed himself). Anyway, he takes a few steps and discovers that what they are given to see is false. It is not Reality but an illusionary representation of it. That's what some people - who hold "power" - want them to see, think and believe.

Quite similarly, what we see on the "wall of our minds" might be what others – television, media, politicians, leaders – wishes us to see, think, believe, consume. Power and Paradigms maintain us in a certain representation of what the world is.

In time, that Reality may become our own preferred television channel. Or we may stop trusting it and prefer to shut down the television set.

Plato's man is called to move on, he climbs up to the exit. He emerges at the surface of the earth, is blinded by the sun, then gets used to light and starts to discover Life: animals, vegetation, minerals and probably other men and women with whom he starts another life.

Then, one day, he remembers where he came from. He remembers the cave and his fellow prisoners. He has the desire to tell them what he has discovered since he left, that there is another world out there.

He goes back into the cave and sits near the men to whom he was chained. He tells them about the Reality outside. He tells them everything about this other world, its beauty, the sun, the animals, the people.

But the others don't believe him.

They say he is crazy.

In his book, "Thus spoke Zarathustra", Friedrich Nietzsche wrote: *"And those who were seen dancing were thought to be insane by those who could not hear the music"*.

The men who remained in the cave cannot hear the music; they cannot imagine another world.

The free man insists. But his Truth disturbs them. It is an "inconvenient Truth".

He becomes a threat to the Reality they are used to believe in.

He becomes a "heretic".

The power threatens him. He is going to be eliminated because he holds another "Truth", another vision of Reality.

What will happen is unknown. But the prisoners have heard him.

The seed is planted, although not visible yet.

And maybe, one day, they will remember and free themselves too.

The free man is the one who knows that he is in chains.

The Future is NO where / NOW here!

#aeroplastics #aliciaeggert

As a Fiction writer declared: *"The Future is already here. It's just not very evenly distributed"*[19].

Consider the French word for Future: l'avenir, literally, "what is yet to come".

It is already somewhere but not visible to our eyes yet!

The Future we imagine is the cause of the Present.

Like the Present, the Future is a "representation", a story we tell ourselves.

As the story of the *Kronberg Castle mentioned earlier* illustrates, an imaginary trace of the Past changes our perception of the Present. In the same way, an imaginary "trace of the Future" also changes our Present!

The Future we imagine exists here and now and has an impact on our current Reality.

It can become the cause of the Present. Or, more accurately, the Future is already the cause of the Present since we all live with an imaginary Future in our mind.

---

[19] *William Ford Gibson (born March 17, 1948) American Canadian speculative fiction novelist*

THE ART OF SHAPERSHIP

At each period of our Life, we tell ourselves a story about our Future, even implicitly, and that story creates an emotional intensity in our Present.

The Future we tell ourselves impacts all aspects of our lives, especially the way we set our priorities and make decisions NOW HERE.

In other words, the Future IS NOW.

More important than that,

The stories of our Future define our Hopes[20]

Why is that? Because what makes Life meaningful is that it has a Future.

And what makes that Life has a future? It is that, at some point, there's something great and awesome that pulls everything else together: Nobility, Dignity, Beauty, Greatness, Elevation: that is the Future.

It is what we crave for, it is what gives meaning to Life.

When we love a person, that's what we want for her/him – the Noble, the Great, and so forth; we want to give that person a Future.

It is what makes Life exciting, what should make a company exciting, what everything should be, because everything should have a Future.

We are ready to go through anything for that.

Insert 3: The notion of Past, Present and Future in Physics

For contemporary Science, that the Future is the cause of the Present is an evidence.

---

[20] *Mark Manson, New York Times and Best-selling Authors*

Great minds like Einstein or Nietzsche had already positioned themselves in the perspective of a Future already realized, that is to say already present somewhere, waiting for us.

Nietzsche asserted that "our Future exerts its influence on us even when we do not yet know it", i.e. in the absence of a memory of the Future. For, according to him, "it is our Future that determines our Present".

Today, illustrious physicists such as Philippe Guillemant and Thibault Damour [21] do not hesitate to affirm that Time does not exist, that the Future is already there, that death is an illusion, and that it is our mind that creates Reality, not the other way around.

According to them, the usual idea of Time passing is an illusion. The real Reality - the veiled Reality - exists within a Space-Time that does not elapse; it is outside of Time. It is to be imagined as packs of cards one on top of the other. The cards are like photographs of the Past, Present and Future, which coexist. As if they were there, simultaneously, but on different frequencies.

As the physicist Philippe Guillemant says:

> *"The future and the past have the same status and the laws of Physics work in both directions of time, as well as causality.*
> *If this new spatial vision of time does not yet reach a true consensus in physics, to the point of raising the awareness of the general public or politics, it is not so much for lack of arguments in its favor - which abound on all sides - as because it comes up against the inertia of a system enclosed by dogmas that perpetuate the old belief, that of a time that*

---

[21] Among modern physicists, Philippe Guillemant, La Route du temps, Ed. Guy Tredaniel, 2014, 37-47, personal translation

> *would preside over the creation in the present of our immediate future. »*[22]

According to Philippe Guillemant, *"Our intentions cause effects in the Future, which become the future causes of an effect in the Present"*. [23]

It is interesting to think that the Future already exists as a potential, i.e. that all the possibilities exist but only some of them will come to materialize and become Reality.

Yet only if we "believe" in those possibilities, in other words if we find them convincing.

Have you noticed, for instance, that people who believe they have bad luck, tend to attract strange things such as a brick that falls on their head? Or that when there are two planes which crash, we say "never two without three", and there is a third crash. Is that normal? Is it just a coincidence or is it that what we believe, even unconsciously, really has an impact on what happens in this unpredictable world?

What happens when we imagine "Apocalypse now"?

What is the meaning of Life today for the people whose vision of the Future is colonized by a belief in an impossibility of Change – an eternal Present – or "Apocalypse now" – the end of the world?

At the opposite, what happens if we can imagine a map of a desirable Future?

What could happen if a significant part of Humanity started to imagine and desire another Future now?

---

[22] Philippe Guillemant, personal translation

[23] Philippe Guillemant and Jocelin Morisson, La Physique de la Conscience, (Ed. Guy Tredaniel, 2015-2016), 37

What type of emotions, decisions, commitments, actions would those visions create?

We are currently going through an immense crisis of imagination which has huge consequences.

In his excellent book, author Adam Arvidson insists on "***Capitalist Realism***": our inability to imagine a Future that is different from the Present.

> *Our times are marked by a pessimism of the Intellect and an optimism of the will, to use an old quote that leftist sometimes throw around. Our Intellectual Pessimism manifest itself in the fact that no one seems to have a serious alternative to our present predicament. Our wilful Optimism means that, despite the absence of alternatives, there is a general desire for change.*
> *I have taken inspiration in the late Mark Fisher essay on "Capitalism Realism". It succinctly spells out and dissects a condition where, as Frederik Jameson originally remarked, "It is easier to imagine the end of the world than to imagine the end of Capitalism!".*[24]

It is a long time ago - long before the COVID 19 pandemic– that this crisis of Imagination began. Our minds have been so deeply "colonised" by the dominant profit-driven worldviews that we are indeed incapable to imagine a different Future to the financial capitalism that reigns, in the Pure Present, with its cyberspace of entrepreneurial Innovation, of commercialized and globalized consumption, where a financial aristocracy

---

[24] Adam Arvidson, "Changemakers. The industrious Future of the Digital economy", (Polity Press, 2019), 1, 8

has taken power, draped in the clothes of Liberalism, to the detriment of the rest of the population.

The problem is precisely that the values of a democratic and civilized Society cannot be strictly financial.

Before Covid-19, there were 60 million more unemployed than in 2007 and today, the perspectives are worse. In many European countries, whole sections of the population are losing Hope, perspectives and points of reference. They are faced with a difficult situation, the outcome of which seems uncertain. The shivers of Growth are an illusion because the real problems have not been identified and solved.

To keep things as they are, there is no need that an immense majority of people - those who desperately need money or those who are able to make money and invest - *believe* in the hegemonic ideology of the system. So that nothing changes, it is enough that they *believe* in its permanence, that they remain unconsciously convinced by the eternity of the system, therefore unable to imagine alternatives of which they themselves are convinced.

But things are in fact going deeper: many young people are completely hopeless, desperate.

They see no Future. Their horizon in the Anthropocene Era is not only the death of all humans: it is the end of the world itself. Dust.

They think "Apocalypse Now", not in the tragic sense of the word "Apocalypses" which means "Revelation" or "Opening" but in a "more than tragic sense": a scientifically heralded and probable end of the world, a meaningless disappearance of humankind.

> *"Every day's existence, particularly for the young, is ever more focused on the present, in a condition of Capitalism realism, where, as Mark Fisher writes: "For most people under*

> twenty in Europe and North America, the lack of alternatives to capitalism is no longer an issue. Capitalism has seamlessly occupied the horizons of the thinkable. Everyday life is lived in a state of "depressive hedonism" where the void of a meaningless existence is filled with "hedonic lassitude" – the easily available micro pleasures of You Tube, fast food, social media and Play Station. Any real change seems impossible.
> (...concerning Frederik Jameson original remark) We no longer mean that hypothetically. The end of the world - as we know it- now seems quite real.
> Why is it so? Why can't we just" change the world", or even, like the revolutionaries of the last turn of the century, **dream** about doing so?"[25]

In what Jonathan Crary describes as "Capitalism 24/7"[26], an entire generation and in fact the entire world, have lost their capacity to dream.

Greta Thunberg, a Swedish activist, in her address to UNO on 23rd September 2019, declared that her dreams and childhood have been stolen from her.

The same has been said by the young French high school students of the Youth for Climate Movement at the occasion of the first strike for the climate:

> "On March 15, 2019, we will join forces with young people around the world for a global strike by students and high school students. We will be called bad students, but those who have not done their duty are the governments

---

[25] Adam Arvidson, page 18

[26] The expression comes from Jonathan Crary: "*24/7: Late Capitalism and the Ends of Sleep*"

> and corporations that are stealing our Future". (...) You too, join the resistance. For this lesson is the most important of all! And this time it is our turn to teach it to the whole world."[27]

Fifteen years before, in 2005, a young man named Florian described the same incapacity to Dream

> "You don't realize what is happening to us. When I speak with young people of my generation, those who are two or three years younger than me, they all say the same thing: we no longer have that dream of starting a family, of having children, a profession, ideals, as you had when you were teenagers; all that is over, because we are convinced that we are the last, or one of the last generations before the end."[28]

The "Nostalgia of the Future"

Luis Barragan, the famous Mexican Architect, once said "Nostalgia is the poetic awareness of the Past", a past forever gone.[29]

Is it possible that, for a lot of young and less young people, a "Nostalgia of the Future" [30] exists?

---

[27] Appeal launched by the young French high school students of the Youth for Climate movement on the occasion of the first strike for the climate on March 15, 2019.

[28] L'impansable (collectif), l'effondrement du temps, Bernard Stigler. Translated b y us

[29] René Burri, Luis Barragan, (Phaidon, 2000), 13

[30] The expression « La Nostalgie du Futur » comes from Jean-Marie le Clézio, « Greta Thunberg, la gravité de la terre », 13 mars 2019

https://www.liberation.fr/planete/2019/03/13/greta-thunberg-la-gravite-de-la-terre_1714887

A "poetic awareness of the Future which is forever gone"?

For them, it is the end of any expectations for the Future, the end of all dreams and of any possibility to realise their dreams.

They are locked into despair.

Greta Thunberg and Youth for Climate speak "in the name of the Living" and if they indeed provoked a sort of Apocalypse, in the sense of an opening, it is because they have broken a shameless silence, forced to stop denial, demanded clarity, responsibility and commitment from adults.

During the manifestations, a sign carried by a young lady read,

> « *You know it's time for change when children act like leaders and leaders act like children*".

The fact that the end of this world is from now on a scientifically probable fact even means that Despair and Tears can become Fear, Rage, Violence, Cynicism, Addiction, and Suicide.

These are what we call Regression Forces. And they won't lead us to a viable and desirable Future.

The same thing is currently happening as a result of the COVID 19 pandemic: a series of companies have gone bankrupt or need to restructure heavily, whereas for some of them, things were going well until then.

Covid has kidnapped their Future. People who are suffering this "rupture" might go panicked or confused, with a certain and implicit "Nostalgia of the Future".

THE ART OF SHAPERSHIP

Creating the "Desire for the Future"

We need to act from the Desire for the Future rather than from the Fear of it.

How can we create a "Desire for the Future"?

How can we escape "Apocalypse Now" and live "No Apocalypse, not now"[31]?

We need Imagination!

Not only that, for sure, but put it first, because it opens possibilities, hence choices, hence Freedom.

We are required to unlock the deep skills of Imagination, Wisdom, Creativity and Reflection.

In fact, we have to develop the ability to change how we think and what we think.

In other words, the Art of Shaping the Future.

Let's start with Imagination.

We are called to believe and to adhere to what Bergson said: "The possible is richer than what is".

We must also dare to dream (even if we all know that, one day or another, that capacity might provoke awaken nightmares).

As an homage to Bernard Stiegler, one of the major thinkers of our times who died on August 6th, 2020, here is an excerpt of his radical prose:

> "In relation with the state of the Planet, people are aware that things cannot go on the way they are and that, if nothing changes, the Planet is doomed.

---

[31] No Apocalypse, Not Now (Full Speed Ahead, Seven Missiles, Seven Missives), Jacques Derrida, Catherine Porter and Philip Lewis, 1984

There are plenty of things to be done but we are governed by depressive morons and Depression can lead to Madness. (...) University scholars are not doing their job, lock themselves in ivory towers and don't manage problems. How come that no one feels concerned by that? We are living in a system of organized cowardice! Hence the need to become involved. We are all exposed to this ordinary madness. Some deny it and pretend they are just fine, but those are the morons, because we all have ups and downs, we are fallible, as Christ proclaims. They deny because they need to convince themselves so they can sleep.

Today it is key to relaunch a **Dream Society.** *Man must dream during the night but must also dream when awake for it is from dreams that emerges the possibility to produce anything new."*[32]

The power of Imagination can help us escape from an eternal Present

Some people despise Imagination, and "dreaming" even more.

But in fact, Imagination is Noble Thinking.

Imagination has a key role to play in these times of Volatility, Uncertainty, Complexity, and Ambiguity. Imagination is **aspirational** by nature: it is the ability to **envision possible Futures** even though the present situation is far removed from that possibility.

It is the ability to have **Transformative Visions,** it gives voices to what is wanting to emerge, to our Hopes and

---

[32] Free translation from an article

Aspirations, it makes the invisible visible, the impossible possible, it opens new paths to the Future.

It is another way of knowing the world, it is learning from the Future. It is shifting our perspectives. It is also another way of learning from ourselves, learning from our deep Aspirations and Inspirations.

As Gaston Bachelard says,

> "Imagination is not only, as the etymology suggests, the ability to form images of reality; it is the ability to form images that go beyond reality. (...) Imagination invents more than things and dramas, it invents new Life, it invents new Spirit; it opens eyes which have new types of vision. It will only see if it has "visions".
> It will have visions if it educates itself with reveries before educating itself with experiences, if the experiences then come as evidence of its daydreams.
> This adhesion to the invisible is the first poetry, it is the poetry that allows us to take taste to our intimate destiny...True poetry is a function of awakening."[33]

That's what we need: to open eyes which have new types of Vision.

The Future, if there is one, must be imagined first.

We are required to think beyond the horizon of the thinkable.

We have to get out of the cave of our representations, to believe that another world is possible and to imagine it.

---

[33] *L'eau et les rêves, essay on the imagination of matter*, Gaston Bachelard,

We need to make alternative and preferred stories of the Future visible, even if they are improbable (impossible to calculate) and then make them achievable.

We call for a narrative able to generate an "erotic" attraction for the Future: one which is based on what makes us truly humane, our deepest Hopes and Aspirations.

Thinking that way is creating the possibility of a bifurcation to an "alternative" Future.

"Creating is resisting", said the great French Philosopher Gilles Deleuze. More precisely, he said, *"Creating is resisting Stupidity"*.[34]

Putting Imagination at work is resisting "Capitalism Realism", the Repetition of the Past, Hopelessness, Fear and Cynicism.

It is resisting the dominant worldviews of Neoliberalism, the "normal" way things are and the story of Scarcity, Separation, Competition, Efficiency, infinite Growth, Power over others, etc. It is not that they are good or bad, but they are just stories: Ideas, Concepts, Things we can decide to question, to challenge and chose to stop to believe.

This of course, is easier when we have created alternative options.

At a time when a discourse unpolluted by "bullshit" comes as a surprise, it is more needed than ever to resist "functional Stupidity" [35] : the incapacity to intelligently mobilise cognitive capacities, an absence of reflexivity, a refusal to use intellectual capacities in other than myopic ways, the incapacity to question evidences, routine approaches, conventional Wisdom that lead us to multiple disasters.

---

[34] L'Abécédaire de Gilles Deleuze, a French documentary produced by Pierre-André Boutang and shot between 1988 and 1989.

[35] A stupidity-Based theory of Organisations, Mats Alesson and André Spicer, Journal of management Studies, 2012

THE ART OF SHAPERSHIP

> *"We argue that functional stupidity is prevalent in contexts dominated by the economy of persuasion which emphasizes images and symbolic manipulation. This gives rise to forms of stupidity management that repress and marginalize doubts and block communicative action."*

In fact, there is an imperative to resist and escape everything that maintains us in our "prisons" or in the cave of our representations: Denial, Ignorance, Dogmatism, Conformism, Fatalism, blind Rationalism, rigid adherence to wishful Thinking.

Insert 4: Regression and Opening forces

This is what is expressed below.[36]

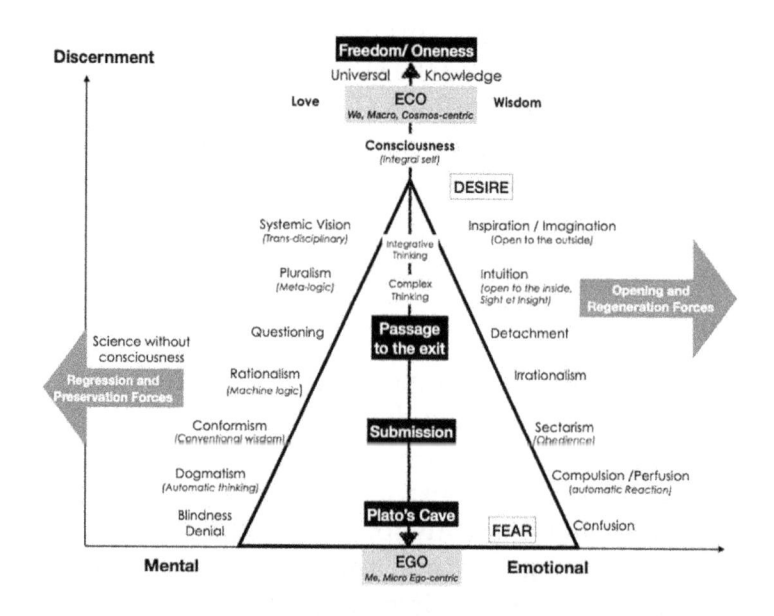

---

[36] Scheme made by Aline, partly inspired by a conversation with Physicist Philippe Guillemant

We move vertically to increase our discernment: from "'Plato's cave" to Submission, to the exit, to Freedom. This is also symbolised by a move from Ego consciousness to Eco-consciousness.

Step by step, we overcome mental and emotional states that limit our discernment to reach more integrative Thinking.

All the stages up to Rationalism and Irrationalism maintain us stuck into the Past.	Once we start questioning what we take for granted and detach ourselves from our habits, we can access new forms of Thinking and knowing such as Intuition and Inspiration.
We are locked into the regression and preservation forces	This is possible thanks to the opening and regenerative forces
1. Fear	1. Courage, Desire and Hope
2. Ego needs	2. Soul Compass and Inner Rightness
3. Lack of Imagination	3. Imagination
4. Conformism and Conventional Wisdom	4. Courage and Unconventional Wisdom
5. Reductionism, Separation, "rigid Rationalism"	5. Broadened perspectives and "integral Thinking"
6. Search for Certainty, Control, Power and Predictability	6. Search for ways to tango with Reality
7. Repetition of the Known	7. Exploration of the Unknown
8. Small and sluggish Thinking	8. Big Thinking as a way to transform Reality

Imagination is one of the main Opening Forces, a force with the immense Power to change Reality, right now, by making counter and preferred stories of the Future "visible".

Those "maps" of the Future become a "lens" through which we reconfigure our "maps" of the Present.

This movement between the Future and the Present is essential and brings us back to the NO WHERE / NOW HERE.

Thinking "radical" and creating the "Erotica of the Future"

Shapership™ is a "Utopia in Action".

The Shapership™ Attitude is radical - A "Big No", a "Big Yes" - in the sense of "back to roots", going to the essence. It is about thinking Big and Radical.

It implies more than just "creating Future possibilities".

It is about taking a stand for "radically different future possibilities", based on completely different worldviews and values.

For Shapership™, the story of the Future is not an "improved" or corrected version of the Present.

The Transformative Vision creates a "perturbation of the Present" because it is a thought of radical difference.

It is a BIG YES to a radically new version of what could be. "*A new model that makes the existing model obsolete*". As we said earlier, instead of trying to "solve the problem", the Shapership™ attitude leads to invent ways to "dissolve it".

Shapership™ implies to "*open new paths towards the Future*", to "*pioneer something*", "*to dream an impossible dream*", to "*open new trails in the jungle of representations*". In short, to shift what people believe is possible in a field that resonates with their Hopes and Aspirations.

The Essence of Shapership™ is the kind of Hope and Desire it generates.

The kind of Future Shapers bring to see because they saw it!

A Shaper actually is what we might call an *"I Opener"*, an *"Eye Opener"*, an "Eye Hopener" and even a *"High Hopener"*.

Because of its radicality, the Transformative Vision has the power of a Utopia.

How?

One of Edgard Morin's thoughts that we (Aline and Jean-Louis) carry in our heart since a long time is the following:

> *"Utopia is at the same time what can change reality and what is incapable of changing it.*
> *Realism is at the same time lucid and blind."*

It implies that Utopia, as a thought of the "impossible" and of radical difference - other place, other time, other space - can have an effect on Reality - although we have to agree on the meaning of this word.

What best describes the strength of the utopian experience is an expression that comes from Habermas: The Future as a disturbance of the Present. It creates a crack in the "imaginary".

Utopia can be seen as the possibility of a radical break with a predicted and colonised Future, as opposed to the belief in an impossible change.

Utopian Imagination opens up new possibilities - or more precisely, it opens up the possibility of new possibilities, - radically different - and therefore, because it takes us out of this inability to imagine a different Future, it also takes us out of the possible "confinement" in a Present assigned to a fixed identity.

A Transformative Vision has the same power to change Reality.

Because it arouses desire.

THE ART OF SHAPERSHIP

There is a "Desire Called Utopia."[37] It is the Desire for the Future.

A Transformative Vision offers a "representation" of the Future which allows others to see it, to believe in it and to aspire to it. Even to stand for it.

Something may call us towards that Future. Something within us creates the Desire to move forward. That's what we have called the "Eros" of the Future.

> *For me, the question is not whether we are sure that the future will be better, the question is whether the advent of a new barbarism is possible. This is the story of the struggle between those who are for union, democracy, brotherhood and those who are for destruction and dislocation, the forces of Eros against those of Thanatos.*
> *I chose Eros. Let's take sides with the good forces because, no matter what happens, in this way we will maintain small oases, islands of resistance. Small lanterns light up in the night, I'm not saying that everything will light up, but it's a good sign.*[38]

Opening "radically" different Futures, the Transformative Vision has a utopian impulse in the sense that Ernst Bloch posits that a utopian impulse governs all that, in life, is turned towards the Future.

---

[37] Frederic Jameson, Archaeologies of the Future: The Desire Called Utopia and Other Science Fictions

[38] The Philosophical Discourse of Modernity: Twelve Lectures (Studies in Contemporary German Social Thought), Jurgen Habermas

Interview of the sociologist and philosopher Edgar Morin, 11th September 2020, https://www.marieclaire.fr/edgar-morin-interview-crise-ecologie-action-citoyenne-coronavirus,1356300.asp?fbclid=IwAR3WiD-QCpe3moRylxEv9Q87_GL4qWbFflYYsIu7ofANfpl_yMhN_iLin3rc

It is an operative Utopia: it produces effect. It opens Time, Space and Matter to "infinite possibilities." It allows to move our head to the other side of the starry vault and see "another Reality". It opens the bubble of the material world and allows to recover our capacity for wonder.

A Transformative Vision, a radical Big Yes" consists in making holes in Time, Space and Matter to let the light of Hope enter.

But, as Einstein said, *"One single ray of light is enough to enlighten a dark room"*.

So, that light also makes us see the current "prison" better: it radically transfigures the Present.

It is a trace of the Future which sends us messages to change our Present.

The Big Yes is that thought of and emotional and "soulful" stand for a radically different Future, in Time and Space, which brings to light whole sections of Present Reality, as if the Present were the shadow of the Future. Having seen other possibilities with the glasses of the Future makes us see, think and feel about the Present differently.

The Present becomes a place of Resistance. It creates a *"devenir révolutionnaire"* - the best translation would be "a revolutionary becoming" [39]. It is a desire, a need, a stand to resist the Present. An attitude which is far from being a capitulation to the Present; on the contrary, it is a rattling of chains shaken by men who are freeing themselves from Plato's cave, an intense spiritual preparation for a Future to come. Provided of course that they are able to hear and BELIEVE that another world is possible instead of seeing it as "an inconvenient Truth".

The result is that, simultaneously, this radical thought creates an attraction for the Future as well as a resistance to the Present.

---

[39] An expression created by the French Philosopher Gilles Deleuze.

THE ART OF SHAPERSHIP

To paraphrase a play on words made by Gilles Deleuze, a French philosopher, about Samuel Butler's utopian fiction, Erewhon, an anagram of the English word Nowhere, which can be read in two ways [40],

- We have a vision of an alternative Future we might "aspire" to: NO WHERE (Out of place)
- Simultaneously, it puts another light on the current Present we might want to "resist" to: NOW HERE!

This is how the Future becomes the cause of The Present.

The Future which is "No Where" becomes a place of Desire "Here and now".

This is how Shapership™ associates the courage of Lucidity with the force of Imagination.

This is the truly revolutionary aspect of the utopian impulse that Shapership™ embodies: it is through its creative radicalism that it reinforces the articulation between the Big No and the Big Yes.

- the Big NO: the refusal of the Déjà-là, of "the" only good way, the negative photo of an unacceptable Present. The awareness of the things that are absolutely revolting and should not exist
- and the big YES: a Beyond, a "Kan sein", as Ernst Bloch said, a "Perhaps that can be" [41], a radically different alternative, oriented towards the fulfilment of historical and collective wishes and which therefore carries the hope of more or less numerous people, in a given historical context. The awareness of what is absolutely desirable and for which we are ready to go through anything.

---

[40] *Erewhon: or, Over the Range*, Samuel Butler (1835-1902).

[41] The principle of Hope, Ernst Bloch

The "Erotica of the Future" is born from this double stance.

It radically impacts the "Theatre of the Mind" and even the "Theatre of the Soul".

This double attraction may confer the density of Passion - and the power to act collectively towards a "Transformative Vision". It is a desire embedded in Love, Dignity, Nobility, Beauty, Greatness, Joy, Compassion and Interconnection. All elements that make Life desirable, exciting and full of Hope.

Hope might be the best path forward. It is the counter-story of all the elements which support the "Regression Forces": Fear, Denial, Despair, Resignation and Cynicism.

> *"Hope is a dimension of the soul and not an objective assessment of a situation.*
> *Hope is not the conviction that something will turn out well but the certainty that something makes sense, regardless of how it turns out."*[42]

In that sense, Shapership™ allows us to escape all forms of reasoning in which Reality is "an excuse not to do".

Paradoxically, the current "Capitalism Realism" - the inability to imagine a different Future -increases, rather than diminishes, the appeal and usefulness of these "Radical Visions".

These types of big thoughts make it possible to think about the Rupture with the Present itself rather than the "eternal" desperating "more of the same".

These "thoughts of the impossible" possess a radical disruptive force: the radicality of the rupture opens the breach towards the Future and sets the transformative imagination in motion.

---

[42] Vaclav Havel, meditation on Hope

Only through radical Thinking, only through super-creative Thinking to the point of Thinking the impossible, can we open a side door through which a Transformative Vision can rush in from the side and create the Erotica of the Future.

Insert 5: No and Yes

We found this No and Yes everywhere.

Starting with the Old Testament, in which the exit from Egypt is told, which we consider here as a metaphorical passage from slavery to inner freedom.

The decisive aspect of the coming out of Egypt - which makes it a revolutionary movement in the integral sense - stems from an immediate articulation

- *of the NO: the destruction of the established order, the rejection of pharaonic oppression and the rejection of the society that made it possible*
- *the YES: the alternative of a different civilization in a state of law that founds the project of another place*
- *Then the passage to synthesis, through the actions of opening and exit*

One of deepest reflections on "Yes" and "No" is found in a famous text: "The three metamorphoses of the mind" Nietzsche talks about in the first chapter of his Zarathustra: "How the mind becomes a camel, how the camel becomes a lion and the lion becomes a child. »

The camel carries the weight of conventional values, of the "you must, you should", of education and culture. He carries them in the desert and there, he transforms itself into a lion.

The lion says a Big No, he breaks the idols, criticizes all values, challenges the "you must, you should".

And then he turns into a child.

Why is this third metamorphosis necessary? Because, says Nietzsche, we need a Big Yes, Yes for the game, Yes for a new beginning, Yes for creating newness. [43]

---

[43] Gilles Deleuze, Nietzsche, (Ed.PUF, 1965), 5

Chapter 3

Who are the Shapers?

Shapers have been around since humans appeared on Earth!

Think about Spartacus, the gladiator from Thrace who changed the life of slaves in Rome.

Think about Toussaint Louverture, head of the Haitian Revolution and major figure of anti-colonialism, abolitionist

THE ART OF SHAPERSHIP

and emancipation movements of black populations in the 18th Century.

Shapers appear in every country, social groups, fields of activity, age-brackets, genders, races and contexts.

In certain cases, Shapers have been asked – or pushed – to become Leaders.

This does not mean that all current Leaders are "Shapers".

Some Leaders are, many are not. Some Entrepreneurs are Shapers, many are not.

Shapers face Reality in creative, visionary and sometimes revolutionary ways.

If Shapers change the world, it is because they make alternative Futures visible. They open new paths for progress that were previously invisible and perceived as "impossible": in Education, Justice, Philosophy, Economics, Health, just to name a few.

Shapers make the Future the cause of the Present.

They make the impossible possible.

They change the story people tell themselves, what they believe is possible or impossible.

Hence, they change people's lives!

We just want to insist on the fact that, in our interconnected world, you don't have to be a Leader or to have a "title" to do something important and have an impact.

You don't have to be someone "important" to take a stand and reshape things.

Anyone with a strong Vision for improving Society and/or their Community can become a Shaper.

Among the more or less famous Shapers of the Past and the Present, we find names like

- Abraham Lincoln (United States 1809-1865): Shaper of a Nation
- Mahatma Gandhi (India, 1869-1948): Shaper of a liberated Nation
- Maria Montessori (Italy 1870-1952): Shaper of a new approach to Education
- Rosa Parks (United States 1913-2005): Shaper of Social Justice and Freedom
- Pastor Jose Maria Arizmendiarrieta (Basque Province of Spain 1915-1976): Shaper of a regional Destiny
- Dr. Govindappa Venkataswamy (India 1918-2006): Shaper of an Eye-Care System with a Vision
- Nelson Mandela (South Africa, 1918-2013): Shaper of Freedom
- Martin Luther King (United States 1929 -1968): Shaper of new Dreams.
- Pierre Rabhi, (1938-): Shaper of a new "Human – Earth Conscience"
- Muhammad Yunus (Bangladesh 1940-): Shaper of Development through Credit for the Poor
- Bernard Lietaer (Belgium, 1942 -): Shaper of the Alternative Currency paradigm
- Daniel Barenboim (Argentina and Israel, 1942-): Shaper of Peace through Music
- Sanjit "Bunker" Roy (India, 1945-): Shaper of Barefoot Education
- Chris Rufer (United States, 1949-): Shaper of Self-Management

- Baltasar Garzón (Spain, 1955-): Shaper of Universal Justice.
- Gunter Pauli (Belgium, 1956-): Shaper of the Blue Economy
- Catia Bastioli (Italy, 1957-): Shaper a new model of Sustainable Development integrated with the territory
- Ricardo Semler (Brazil, 1959-): Shaper of Industrial Democracy
- Michel Onfray (France, 1959-): Shaper of Freedom of Thought through Philosophy
- Rob Hopkins (United Kingdom, 1968-): Shaper of the Transition Town Movement
- Vishen Lakhiani (United States, Malaysia 1976-): Shaper of Self-Development for all
- Salman Khan, Bengali, (1976 -): Shaper of Education for Many
- Jack Andraka (United-States, 1997 -) Shaper of a new cancer detection test

In this book, we tell the story of some of them in more details. Their approach to Life may be an inspiration for everyone.

Shapers have the capacity to get out of the cave of dominant "representations", and to inspire others to free themselves.

Shapers don't consider the shadows on the wall as "Reality".

Their perspective puts another light on the world.

They think big, they have transformative and radical Visions that resemble Utopias, and which open up time, space and matter to let Hope in.

They are not prisoners of facts and appearances. They are not captured by the dominant stories, taken for granted ideas and worldviews of their time.

They are not under the pressure to conform.

They usually are "Maverick Souls" [44], determined to serve the World by bringing significant, seemingly impossible and durable changes.

They see things from an Eco-System Consciousness of Reality, way beyond any Ego-System Awareness.

Shapers have faith in an alternative Future which includes their Hopes and Aspirations. Something that may seem "impossible": a Vision of a radically different Future, sometimes a Utopia, "a dream to make come true".

They know it is not going to be easy, but Shapers want this "impossible possible" to become Reality.

Their Faith and their Hopes become their drive.

After all, miracles are things that are impossible from an old understanding of reality and possible from a new one.

Shapers know that the famous sentence "*I only believe what I see*" should be reversed. And they reverse it!

Shapers know that "*The eye only sees what the brain is ready to understand*".

They have visions which open new eyes.

They see tomorrow's Reality. They see future possibilities and believe in them.

They see what they believe in. And they make it a Reality that changes Reality.

---

[44] Thanks to Sidney Poitier for coining the expression in his speech to the American Film Institute at his Life Achievement Award in 1991.

THE ART OF SHAPERSHIP

While the doubter is busy doubting, telling himself *"I only believe what I see"*, the Shaper is busy making the Future happen: *"I see what I believe"* then, *"I create what I believe"*.

The Essence of Shapership™ is Hope.

Hope made visible because it is displayed!

Shapers are "Eye-Openers", "Eye Hopeners" and "High Openers" because they open Visions and new reasons for hoping!

Shapers open meaningful and progress-generating trails for the whole human "Eco-system", trails that people may desire to follow.

Shapers dare *"The Age of Unreason", as described by Charles Handy, an Irish author/philosopher specialising in organisational behaviour and management:*

> *"We are entering an Age of Unreason, a time when the Future, in so many areas, is to be shaped by us and for us; a time when the only prediction that will hold true is that no prediction will hold true; a time, therefore, for bold imagining in the private life as well as public; for thinking the unlikely and doing the unreasonable."* [45]

But their road is often paved with obstacles and difficulties.

The more the trail they open may potentially disrupt the conventional models, the more they generate resistance. And the larger their scope of influence, the stronger the resistance. So, the "success" of their story is not measured by the smoothness of their path, nor by the quantitative and short-term results they obtain, but by the importance – sometimes the irreversibility – of the transformations

---

[45] Charles Handy "The Age of Unreason ", 1989

they bring to Society and to the world, during their lifetime and beyond.

The changes brought by Shapers become their heritage. A lasting heritage that cannot be reduced to measurable quantities. The gift Shapers bring to the world goes far beyond the mere level of facts and way beyond their own lifetime. It goes beyond their control. In fact, beyond anybody's control. Their actions resonate long after they happened.

We cannot say, incontrovertibly, that any one Shaper has permanently changed a situation for the better as a result of his or her actions, e.g. Martin Luther King has not totally eliminated social injustice and racism; Judge Balthasar Garzón has not eliminated corruption, terrorism or dictatorships despite his lifetime commitment to eradicating them.

What we can say is that Society, as a whole, has changed. Many - not all - of the tensions and revelations of Society today, in 2020, represent the playing-out of forces that the Shapers unveiled a certain time ago, way back in the 1960's or 1950's for some, much longer for many.

Even if, in the meantime, Shapers have died or "accidentally" lost their reputation or their Freedom, their heritage belongs to Humanity. They generate "Cultural Revolutions".

Shapers are History Makers.

Although it often starts at the individual level, with a Shaper or a group of Shapers, Shapership™ can become a collective capacity as it did with "The Equitable Pioneers of Rochdale", one of the first consumers cooperatives founded in 1844 in England by 28 Lancashire weavers or, more recently, the Transition Town Movement. Since the Shapers create "Movements", each embedded in a specific period in History, we can say that each person who freely makes the choice

THE ART OF SHAPERSHIP

of actively participating and contributing to the "Cause" becomes a Shaper. "Power to the Shapers".

Insert 6: Transgression and Transmission

As it implicitly appears from what has been said so far, Shapers adopt a new approach to Life, to Freedom, to Work, to Power, to Consumption and to Humanity, to the Heritages received and the one transmitted.

Transgression is at the heart of the Shapers attitude.

In the film Lawrence of Arabia, a movie by David Lean, Lawrence decides to turn back and search for a man lost in the desert. Cherif Ali (played by Omar Sharif) tells him:

- "But, Lawrence, you will not find this man. It is impossible. It is written".

To what Lawrence, hitting his forehead with his stick answers:

- "Nothing is written, Ali, except here!"

Neither the Past, nor the Present, nor the Future can become the "Prisons" of our Mind"! A great Alchemist of our time, Patrick Burensteinas, says this: there are two ways of living our Life: either to improve our incarceration, or get out of our prison. It takes courage to get out.

Shapers ignore "Fatalisation". They transgress taken-for-granted assumptions and situations. They get out.

Transmission, and thus the notion of exemplarity, is also at the core of Shapership™. To fully understand the meaning of the word, we should read it: Trans-Mission:

- beyond one's own mission.

    The Shaper is at the service of "more" - other people or groups, a field, a region, a country, Humanity, the World.

The Shaper does what she/he has to do, guided by her or his deep personal Awareness, Presence, Intention and Attention which are beyond any Ego System.

A Shaper's Eye, Heart, Soul and Spirit are connected to their body and to the world. She/he looks further than the tip of the nose and always in harmony with important issues of her/his time.

A Shaper goes beyond one's own desire while including it!

A Shaper carries the hopes of many people. Her/his Life Mission is not "personal" but beyond her/his own person and Ego. It is "transpersonal".

Martin Luther King's "I have a Dream" has opened the hearts of millions of people. Even if, as somebody who did not understand what Shapership™ is said: "It didn't do him any good!".

Maybe not, but he changed the world!

- beyond "Here and Now".

Shapership™ is long-term Thinking, meaning- making of the Past, the Present and of the Future we create for ourselves and the people we relate to. It leads to a "Cultural Revolution", to Progress or to a Movement.

Chapter 4

The DNA of Shapership™

"The Altitude Attitude" © and the "Soul Compass"

How do Shapers make alternative and meaningful Futures Visible and actionable?

As a State of Being and of Consciousness, Shapership™ invites a series of personal alignments and connections.

Shapers have what we call *"the Altitude Attitude"*©!

- They have a helicopter vision and yet are totally in tune with the world. They "tango" with Reality and wonder what should happen to meet the real issues and needs

- Their perspective rises above the Ego and any conservative movement

- They connect Head, Heart and Hands

This integrity of the Being based on a full connection between an Open Mind, an Open Heart and an Open Will [46] is what gives Shapers the capacity to see / think BIG AND RADICAL.

At this point, we need to keep in mind that the word "radical" does not mean "extremist". It actually means sticking to the essence, the principle (of somebody, something) and having the desire to act upon the deep roots of what one wants to change.

As a practice, Shapership™ derives its transformative impact from the coherent articulation of three very simple elements [47] that all Shapers activate, as anyone can do in his/her everyday life

1. Creative Resistance: The Big "NO"
2. Transformative Vision: The Big "YES"
3. Anticipative Experimentation: The Creative "HOW"

It is worth noticing that these three leverages may seem like "a process to follow" or a protocol.

They are in a way, yet they are much more than that.

First, they don't happen in linear sequence in time. But they need to be fully "alive" and connected to create a self-reinforcing loop.

Second, these three "leverages" - we will describe in more details - are nothing without "Spirit". They only mean something if they are activated and "animated" by the full connection between an open Mind, an Open Heart and an Open Will.

---

[46] Otto Sharmer, senior lecturer at the Sloan School of Management MIT, co-founder of the Presencing Institute, inventor of "Theory U"

[47] The 3 elements mentioned here are inspired by Patrick Viveret, « La cause humaine. Du bon usage de la fin d'un monde », ed. Les Liens qui Libèrent. Nevertheless, we took the liberty to broaden their meaning

That's what we call that the *"Soul Compass"* – take it as a magnetic compass for orientation or a drawing compass to have a fixed point from which to open to the world. The "Soul Compass" is our inner Consciousness, based on another way of knowing, which allows to hear all our voices – see with our eyes, feel with our Heart, follow our Intuition - , to develop inner rightness, to find the force to "take a stand" against and for something, to explore the unknown with Courage and Imagination.

Therefore, we say that the Shapership™ Attitude is not abstract and egocentric; it emerges from our inner *"Soul Compass"* which deeply "knows":

1. That the "way things are" needs to be challenged": status quo must be resisted as well as our "Routine Thinking". This leads to the Big "NO": the Creative Resistance

2. That another and more beautiful "world" is possible, that *"what is possible is richer than what is"*. [48]

    This leads to the Big "YES": the Transformative Vision

3. That a Transformative Vision calls for transformative Actions and that it will require Courage to completely reinvent the way things operate and to shift from one paradigm to another. That's what we call the Creative "HOW": the Anticipative Experimentation.

---

[48] Henri Bergson, French Philosopher

Insert 7: the "Altitude Attitude" ©

The Transformative Vision: the Big "YES"
See Reality "as it could be" and open new paths to the Future

The Creative Resistance: the Big "NO"
See Reality "as it is" and challenge the status quo

The "Altitude Attitude"
3 elements to connect in a self-reinforcing loop

The Anticipative Experimentation: the Creative "HOW"
Reinvent ways things operate, with a dynamic ecosystem of committed partners

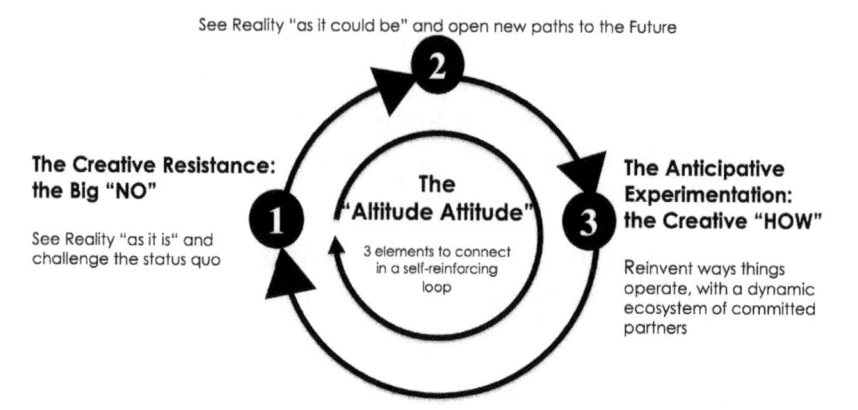

When connected in a self-reinforcing loop, these elements form the "DNA" of Shapership™ and create the Transformative Impact.

Let's look at each of them first.

1. Creative Resistance: The Big "NO"

Creative Resistance is the Art of Seeing and Sensing.

It is above all a way of Seeing (and Listening to) Reality "as it is" with fresh "lenses", understanding and making sense versus downloading old maps, shifting perceptions and challenging the Status Quo.

It is making the limits of the current system visible – an organization, a family, a way of life – and the signs that it is not viable for the Future.

Shapers see the way things are (Business as Usual or "normal) with liberated minds. They look at Reality square in the face and feel a deep and sincere "NO" to any "taken-for-granted" situation seen as "normal" by a vast majority of people.

In fact, Shapers are "pissed off" by the status quo: they believe it must be disrupted.

They see and sense from the field the latent needs for a new Reality to take shape.

They want "more" or "something else". They see current Reality as a state of Evolution, which, for the sake of Humanity, needs to be "upgraded" to a new level. To them, accepting the status quo would be like accepting to remain in a form of "Middle Ages".

And Dark Ages call for a "Renaissance".

Shapers sense that, from the dark, something is trying to find its way to the Light. That something wants to be born. Something that means Hope for a better World. Value for Many!

Something in tune with global imperatives and true "demands".

Creative Resistance is an inside-out resistance to "Imprisonments" of all kinds: "clichés", habits, conventional Wisdom, "Old Guard" principles, obsolete assumptions such as *"It is the only and best way to do"*, or excuses for not doing before even knowing what to do.

If we take the metaphor of the iceberg, Shapers look at what is above and under the surface. They observe the visible world, above the surface: the dominant and conventional actors, structures, approaches, way of living. They see and understand the broader context: the strategic landscape, the global challenges, the economic system, the power games, the forces at play.

Crucially, the Shapers also look at the submerged part of the iceberg – which is the most important as you know. They make the invisible visible: the current mental maps. Shapers identify the taken for granted beliefs, ideas and assumptions that might keep themselves or a situation "stuck". They make the water we are swimming in visible.

And they examine how they themselves are shaped by these stories, how they obey them and how they keep them alive through their own decisions and actions.

Shapers are aware of how they contribute to maintaining the old or to shaping a new world.

Just by "looking" at Reality in a fresh way, a Shaper is already escaping the Prison of the Known, of facts, prejudices and mindsets. She or he initiates a creative deconstruction of "what is" and a creative reconstruction of "what is possible". The Shaper becomes a new kind of Pioneer. She or he represents the "Unsung Voice" of many or the "Dormant Conscience" of Humanity. The Shaper becomes the symbol of the Changes some people want to see happen in the world.

This attitude is called "Creative Resistance" because it is more than a "reaction" to an external event. It is not a "Revolt" nor an act of Despair. It is more of a "Protest" and a "Let's start a Revolution" stance. Creative Resistance drives the Shaper to take a stand and to start a transformation. This leads to Transgression, positive Deviance or Disruption.

Creative Resistance is a durable "attitude" but is not enough just by itself. As the great scientist and futurist, Buckminster Fuller once said:

> *"You never change things by fighting the existing Reality. To change something, build a new model that makes the existing model obsolete".*

A Transformative Vision is needed.

2. Transformative Vision: The Big "YES"

Shapers are pioneers. They are trailblazers, opening possible paths into the Future. At first, these paths are invisible to others - like new trails in the jungle no one would see nor dare to tread until they are opened.

Because they are not imprisoned in the cave, chained with facts, appearances or representations, Shapers dare a creative reconstruction of Reality "as it could be".

They unlock their Imagination and see with broader perspectives. They make alternative stories of the Future visible. They dare to think big, to "envision" radically different and desirable Futures that might be created.

This transformative Vision becomes a "Meaning-Making Story" of the Future. It may range from "Utopia" to "Dream", [49] to "Purpose"[50], to a "Stance" [51]. which enhances the Dignity, the Nobility and the Significance of Human Life.

This Transformative Vision emerges from the Shapers interaction with the grounded Reality of what is needed in the world. It is a helicopter view in tune with Reality. It emerges from the deep interaction between the Shapers and the real issues at stake in the world.

These are super ambitious goals grounded in what needs to be done to solve ecosystem issues.

As David Bohm, one of the remarkable Quantum physicists of all times, puts it:

> *"If it has Meaning, it has Value.*
> *It can then become a Purpose".*

---

[49] See Martin Luther King

[50] See Dr. Govindappa Venkatasmy who founded Aravind Eye-Care System in 1976 in India to "Eliminate Needless Blindness", or Tesla's purpose as Elon Musk puts it: "Accelerate the worlds transition to sustainable energy"

[51] See Rosa Park

The Transformative Vision that Shapers embody expands the limits of what is possible and of what people believe is possible. It radically shifts the way themselves and others make sense of Reality. It opens new paths towards the Future. The Future becomes a "lens" which helps focus attention on new shapes of Reality that can be created. The Future then becomes the cause of the Present, it is a "Cause" people want to serve and contribute to.

The Transformative Vision becomes an **aspiration** which has meaning beyond themselves.

It touches people's souls because it meets their desires, needs and aspirations.

It symbolizes a fairer world. When it is "embodied" in the most authentic way, the power of the Transformative Vision leads to the creation of an irreversible movement.

It allows to disrupt the system with a Purpose.

The big YES is not a platitude, it is an attitude. It is at the same time the vision of a meaningful Future that can be created AND a deep commitment to make it happen.

It is not a rational statement of what should happen. It is the response Shapers give to a call, from within their full Presence and Awareness. It is the opposite of a hollow statement just made of words. It is an existential stance, a state of being in the world characterized by a full connection between Mind, Heart and Will.

Their Transformative Vision is a big "Yes" to a NO-MAD or less MAD world, a reshaped Reality (within a more or less extended scope and scale). It drives revolutionary and pioneering Wealth-Creation (cultural, societal, economic, intellectual, emotional...).

The Values embedded in the Purpose are highly humane and transcend all the petty boundaries of the Ego, colour, gender, country as well as usual Business goals such as "out-perform or even kill the competition".

Shapers are not only involved; they are committed to make changes happen.

Who they are and what they do embody the changes they want to see happen, and more often, a shift in Paradigm.

They put themselves "at the service" of their Vision which becomes the axis on which they align their thoughts and actions to courageously venture into the Unknown in spite of all possible difficulties, ambiguities and uncertainties.

It gives them the drive to overcome fear and difficulties. It is their guiding Force, the "Will" emanating from their true Self, their source of Courage, the stance of Nobility and Dignity everyone yearns for.

By being who they are, they indicate a direction and a way to "craft" Reality. They don't only talk; they walk their talk. They practice what they preach. They shape and are shaped by their Transformative Vision.

Shapers irradiate Authenticity and Integrity.

To paraphrase the Japanese proverb:

> *"A Vision without Action is an awaken dream.*
> *But Action without Vision is a nightmare"*,

We can say that a Transformative Vision without Resistance and Experimentation remains an awaken dream, without concrete applications.

3. Anticipative Experimentation: The Creative "HOW"

The Transformative Vision calls for Transformative actions, in a coherent way, to embody the Future.

Now that there is a Vision of a radically different Future, how are we going to get there? How are we going to make it happen - to make this Future a reality and not an ersatz version? How are we going to avoid crashing it all? How are we going to deal with the tensions between the "world as it is" and the Future we want?

This is the ideal moment to use the word "Transition" in a proper way: make visible a path that allows to "navigate" and shift from one pattern of activity to a radically desirable one.

It is not about making a "plan", making compromises or using Reality as an excuse.

It is not the moment to correct the Past or maintain the current system in place, in the name of Fear, lucid Realism, short termism or conventional recipes.

It is neither the moment to pretend that "we make change happen" in the right direction whether everyone can see that the so-called disruptive answers we bring do not fundamentally challenge the values and goals that are becoming more and more unsustainable. They might indeed be more efficient, but they are not transformative.

Anticipative experimentation is the bold path to navigate the transition and the dilemmas, without remaining prisoner of the existing paradigm.

Guided by the Transformative Vision, Shapers think and act with a radically different Future in Mind. This extended perspective opens the space for Transformative Innovation.

Shapers escape the current paradigm to actively shape viable and exciting Futures in the long-term.

They disrupt a system with a purpose.

They open trails and follow them, persuaded that "*it is never impossible. It is just harder*".

They generate new forms of Reality such as "Life reinvented", "Work reinvented", "Power reinvented", "Strategy reinvented", "Mobility reinvented", "Love and Compassion reinvented". Indeed, to move to action and shape new realities, Shapers usually completely reinvent the way things work. They escape the established rules, practices and organizations which usually don't welcome changes of such magnitude.

Anticipative Experimentation means exploring and "Learning by Doing". It is the transformative path towards a new Reality, thanks to the appropriate set of strategies, approaches and actions that fully embody the Vision and make it happen in a coherent way.

And Shapers need perfect alignment because their actions create resistance. Exactly like what the man who escaped from "Plato's Cave" experienced.

The Shapers' purpose is sometimes so ambitious that some people think they are completely megalomaniac! (a person who is obsessed with their own power). For others, such as those locked in the repetition of the "S.O.S." (Same Old Solutions) or the established "authorities" (whether official, corrupted, or not, dictators or not, or simply the dominant conventional Wisdom-keepers), Shapers represent such a threat to their "turf", their security, or their certainties that they try to "eliminate" them.

And not always in the most elegant ways: assassinations, imprisonments, calumnies, destructions of reputation, denials, moving them away. Sometimes, they succeed – think of Martin Luther King, Gandhi, Nelson Mandela, Muhammad Yunus, Baltasar Garzón and many others.

One thing is certain: the strength and the magnitude of the resistance, the regression forces or even the violence that Shapers face are proportionate to the dangers they "represent" for the powers in place. The bigger the issue, the closer "Death" gets!

Fortunately, Shapers also have "supporters", those who are moved by who they are and the purpose they embody. The path opened and made visible by the Shapers deeply resonate with their soul, as if it had always been their aspiration.

It also holds their hopes. They choose to walk the new trails. One after the other, they create a Movement and bring Collective Change about.

Shapers are "Ecosystem-Aware" and their purpose is to have an impact on systems larger than themselves. Therefore, they develop Ecosystem strategies. Because they know system issues require system solutions, Shapers abolish Competition and create new forms of Collaboration.

They envision creative ways to make Change happen. They creatively imagine how they can remove the obstacles of all kinds which prevent their "Purpose" and "Value Proposition" to be fully delivered to those who need them. Therefore, they create and rally a formidable Ecosystem of committed Actors, Partners and Complementors. [52]

Anticipative Experimentation is really the place for co-creation – it requires alliances, including with Life itself, to create new realities. True co-creation demands unconventional ways to deal with notions such as Control, Power, Trust, Freedom, Responsibility, Competition and Collaboration. In fact, it requires whole new ways of exploring the Humanity within us.

Shapers share Power, because for them, there is no Top nor Bottom, no levels, no competition. There is a Cause.

Shapers don't act alone, especially in this networked age. They create new forms of collaboration. We are not talking

---

[52] As examples, see further, Dr. V. for Aravind Eye-Care System and Catia Bastioli with Novamont

about social networks here. We are talking about "work-nets": " Communities of Souls", people, partners and "adopters" who join an ecosystem because they want to be part of the adventure. It can be a "movement", a "company", a "community"...it will be a "work-net" of commitments around a Purpose (not around a guru).

New organizational models are in line with that Spirit. They are more horizontal, participative, collaborative, playful.... up to a point where their design perfectly fits with what they are: a leverage for Transformation.

These "organizations" have replaced the old contradiction between "Order" or "Disorder" with a **maximum of two principles: Focus AND Freedom.**

Metaphorically, they are closer to Jazz combos (combination of musicians) than to classical hierarchical Symphony Orchestras:

- **Focus**: knowing what "piece to play", at what tempo, in what key...which metaphorically in an organization, means agreeing on all the factors which create Cohesion: a Vision, an Intention, a Strategy, Values, just to name some.

- **Freedom**: Jazz is based on "Improvisation within a harmonic Structure", on Creativity in Real Time, on permanent Learning, Exploration, constant Listening and Fun.

These organizations – sometimes called "liberated" - innovate organically within a "Purpose orientation".

They are well-balanced and at the service of a higher purpose, not of Control, or Risk Management or Profit maximization.

These "organizations" transform their "members" into "Peers" and "Shapers". They are designed to ensure maximum Learning, Experimentation and Agility, encouraging all

THE ART OF SHAPERSHIP

members at all levels to see, think, innovate and act in new ways. Work becomes a dynamic process of Knowledge-Creation and Innovation, thanks to the development of a new Art and Science of Collaboration.

As you will discover in the following examples, the core of Shapership™ is about Power exerted "with others" - not on Power exerted "over others" – and about shared Focus (Purpose), Freedom (including Freedom of Commitment) and Responsibility. [53]

The "Music" of Shapership™: articulation for Transformative Impact

As the famous conductor Daniel Barenboim says: *"The purpose of Music is Integration: it integrates the whole in harmony"*.

Moving from "fixed" scores to "harmony" requires the music to be played: *"Play the music, not the notes"*[54]

The "Music" of Shapership™ is the activation of the strong articulation between its three pillars: Creative Resistance, Transformative Vision and Anticipative Experimentation, inhabited at their core by the "Altitude Attitude", maintained by the open "Soul Compass".

Not as an abstract and rational exercise, disconnected from reality, dominated by "Ego Needs", the desire to control, predict, win over, defeat, eliminate, kill, sell more and make profits endangering the Planet.

On the contrary, the Altitude Attitudes allows to shape the Future from a deeply open and integrated perspective, connecting

---

[53] This will be illustrated by several cases, among others in the Business world by Chris Rufer, Ricardo Semler and Vishen Lakhiani

[54] Attributed to Miles Davis

- Vision and Action, Heads, Hearts and Hands: opening the "soul compass" way beyond Ego-awareness and being open to other way of knowing,

- Inside and Outside, Ego and Eco awareness: finding the inner rightness while keeping the eyes wide open, serving the Fabric of Life

- People to the "Vision" and action in ways that escape domination and power over others: bringing the Big Picture to Life and share it so that each person "owns" it, creating ecosystem approaches based on Focus and freedom

- Past, Present and Future, with renewed perspectives: enlarging and deepening the awareness of things as they are and as they are becoming, avoiding denial and "the "ostrich" syndrome as well as *fatalisation* and *conformation* of any sort.

This is Shapership™ as a practice to change the stories that shape our lives, so we can change the way we shape the Landscape.

Playing the notes but not the Music

When they are badly connected, they certainly do not generate the same impact.

Why?

For at least three reasons:

1. Creative Resistance without a Transformative Vision will lead nowhere, except to Revolt and/or Despair.

2. Vision needs forms of Anticipative Experimentation to "make it happen", to materialise and embody its transformative aspects.

3. Anticipative Experimentations which are disconnected from the Creative Resistance and the Transformative Vision lose both their subversive and their aspirational aspects.

Let's look at the first point: Creative Resistance disconnected from a Transformative Vision.

It does not generate Hope nor Desire.

It obeys a logic of Despair, Impotence, Depression or Fear.

A good example is the famous Sidney Lumet movie, "Network".

It is about a fictional television network, Union Broadcasting System's (*UBS)* and its struggle to get better ratings.

It tells the story of Howard Beale, the long-time star of UBS evening news program. One night, he learns from his friend and News Division President Max Schumacher that, because of poor ratings, he has just two more weeks on the air. The night after, Howard Beale announces during his show that he will commit suicide live, during a next broadcast. This is not appreciated by UBS and he is fired. But he obtains from his friend Schumacher to appear one last time on TV to leave in a dignified manner. Beale promises to apologize but instead, once on the air, he explains that *"he simply ran out of Bullshit"* and that *"Life is bullshit"*.

The ratings explode and the upper echelons of UBS decide to exploit Beale's rage, offering him more occasions to be on the air.

One of the most famous scenes of the movie is Beale's live monologue - which might resonate with what many people feel today – expressing a galvanizing "Big No":

> "I don't have to tell you things are bad. Everybody knows things are bad.

It's a depression. Everybody is out of work or scared of losing their job.
The dollar buys a nickel's worth; banks are going bust, shops keep guns under the counter, punks are running wild in the street and there is no body that seems to know what to do and there is no end to it.
We know the air is unfit to breathe and our food is unfit to eat.
We sit watching our TV while some local news casts tell us that today we had 15 homicides and 63 violent crimes, as if that's the way it's supposed to be!
We know things are bad! Worse than bad: they are crazy! It's like everything everywhere is going crazy.
So, we don't go out anymore. We sit in the house and slowly the world we are living in is getting smaller. And all we say is please, please, at least leave us alone in our living rooms. Let me have my toaster, my TV and my radio and I won't say anything. Just leave us alone!
Well! I am not going to leave you alone. I want you to get mad.
I don't want you to protest, I don't want you to write to the congressman because I wouldn't know what to tell you to write. I don't know what to do about the depression or the inflation, and the Russians and the crimes in the streets.
All I know is that first, you got to get mad. You got to say: I'm a human being, my life has value, God damn it!"

At this moment, he stands up and says several times:

THE ART OF SHAPERSHIP

> *I want all of you to get out of your chairs now,*
> *I want you to stand up and go to the window,*
> *open it, stick your head out and yell:*
> *I Mad as hell and I am not gonna take this any-more."*

The "success" is huge. In every city, people are going to their window and yell: *I am Mad as hell and I am not gonna take this any-more."*

You can watch the scene here [55] and feel the jubilation.

It is the jubilation of a Big NO.

But as Sydney Lumet himself says about his movie: nothing has changed after that scene, at least nothing fundamental in "people's life".

It all stayed "in the box", a TV "Reality show".

Howard Beale did not quit his job, an entire TV show was created for him to express his rage, huge audiences came to listen to *The Howard Beale Show* (live and on the air), applauding at the end of each sermon at the moment where he vanishes.

And nothing changed. Until people got tired of his sermon, audiences scores diminished, he made a mistake and he had to be eliminated. UBS executives hired someone to assassinate Beale during his live show. He got shot on the air and when he fell, the audience applauded.

Of course, Network is a movie made in 1976 about television and about people "who sometimes have grown up for three generations with TV reality, without reading books."

But 50 years later, it sounds like a prophecy. Not only about television. But also, about a certain inertia of an entire society

---

[55] Network, "I'm mad as hell speech, https://youtu.be/q_qgVn-Op7Q

which may have partly grown up in its ability to say a Big No but continues to be enslaved and lobotomised, reduction of the mental or emotional capacity or ability to function of, by less and less credible dominant medias and worldviews.

Anyway, a Big No without a Big Yes has no Transformative Power.

Nicknamed *"The man who repairs women"*, Doctor Denis Mukwege has received numerous awards for his commitment against female genital mutilation in the Democratic Republic of Congo, including the Sakharov Prize in 2014 and the Nobel Peace Prize in 2018.

He certainly is a remarkable man.

But the fact is that, as he tells, one day he realized he was taking care of the daughters of the women he took care of years before. The infernal cycle had not stopped, things had not changed.

What we observe is that he certainly said a big No and made a remarkable job. But, unless we are wrong, he did not say a Big Yes: he did not propose a Transformative Vision of a radically different Future. He repaired women, he solved problems, case by case, but he did not open up the system to an alternative path that would make the previous system obsolete.

As you will see in the following pages, a Big No with a Big Yes is creating a reinforcing impact on both the Big No and the Big Yes.

Think of Pierre Rabhi "Happy Sobriety" as a way of living.

Sobriety is not fun. It might be a fair resistance to over consumption, addiction or waste – some major symptoms that indicate a "malaise" in our Society - but Sobriety doesn't evoke anything festive. And by the way, it only addresses the visible symptom- the excessiveness; Not its cause, the pain of living.

The positive couple "Happy Sobriety" evokes the idea of another Lifestyle - live well. It includes an idea of Joy and Pleasure which can generate Desire.

The Second reason why the three leverages need to be connected is easy to understand: a Transformative Vision needs forms of Anticipative experimentation to "make it happen", to materialise and embody its transformative aspects. Without that Transition Path made visible, it remains an Aspiration. Although as we said, it is also a source of Hope, since it produces a "No Where/ Now Here" effect, it might well increase the feeling of being "stuck" in the Present for too long.

This is why we need to find encouragements in the Present. Whatever we are "dreaming of" for the Future, there are always living demonstrations, somewhere in the world, that it is possible. Someone has already talked about it, some others are already doing it, entirely or partially. We can get inspiration from those examples; we can be nurtured by those evidences that what we are hoping for is possible. And we can connect with them to learn from them. This is true at the individual and at the collective level.

Finally, let's see how Anticipative Experimentations lose their subversive and their aspirational aspects when they are disconnected from Creative Resistance and Transformative Vision.

Take the example of Micro Credit for the Poor (which will be developed later).

Muhammad Yunus a social entrepreneur, banker, economist, and civil society leader who was awarded the Nobel Peace Prize said a "Big No" to the system which excluded many people from accessing money. He resisted completely to all the arguments of the Macro Credit.

He had the Vision of Micro – or nano- credit as a leverage for transforming Society.

And he made it happen through the Grameen bank.

Beware of imitations! What is happening now in many European countries?

Incumbent banks practice Micro Credit for the Poor, without any Creative Resistance nor Transformative Vision.

They have kidnaped the concept to support their own "business model", and Micro-credit now allows more rich people to make money thanks to poor people.

Disconnected from the two other leverages, the Transformative Impact almost disappeared. Micro credit becomes a niche market for dominant actors, a sort of ethical Green Washing, locked in the old paradigm of Value capture.

The same is true for the most part of the Bio market. It has lost its initial subversive power and has been kidnapped by the major retailers to "capture" a growing "niche market".

Think of Fairtrade. It was designed as a resistance to unfair working conditions for producers (mainly cocoa and café) and as a way to move from distributive to Generative Justice [56]:

> *In Marxist frameworks "distributive justice" depends on extracting value through a centralized state. Many new social movements—peer to peer economy, maker activism, community agriculture, queer ecology, etc.—take the opposite approach, keeping value in its unalienated form and allowing it to freely circulate from the bottom up. Unlike Marxism, there is no general*

---

[56] Ron Eglash, of Marx and makers: an historical perspective on generative Justice, technokultura, 13.03.2016

theory for bottom-up, unalienated value circulation.

This is the concept of "Generative Justice": one in which society is best served when value extraction is minimized, and when the communities who are generating value—not Adam Smith's capital or Marx's state—are in charge of its circulation.

If we phrase this in the language of "rights"— which is not the only way to think about it--we can define Generative Justice as follows:

- *The universal right to generate unalienated Value and directly participate in its benefits;*
- *the rights of value generators to create their own conditions of production;*
- *and the rights of communities of value generation to nurture self-sustaining paths for its circulation.*

Disconnected from a Transformative Vision, Fair Trade (for instance in Cocoa) is now captured by dominant industrial actors. They instrumentalise it for greenwashing purposes, to appear as "Conscious Businesses" while they in fact maintain the old Value capture model which fits their interests, maximising their profit and "redistributing" almost insignificant parts to producers.

It is worth looking at any "Anticipative Experimentation" by connecting it to its "roots", both in the "Creative Resistance" and in its Vision. For instance, "Slow Living" is an interesting way to resist the acceleration of Time - "Time Poverty" as it is called -, the infernal cadences, the 24/7 online mode of life, the slavery of deadline for so-called emergencies and stress. It is a calling *"Stop the world I want to get off!"*

The "Slow Living Movement" proposes a transformative Vision: it aspires to a different relationship to time, appreciating simple things, creating new connections and a good life. The "Slow Living Movement" gave birth to a lot of Experimentations: Slow Food, Slow Cities, Slow Living, Slow Schools, all nurtured by its inspirations and aspirations. And then, what happened? Experimentations started without connections to those roots. And those "slow" initiatives became "fashions" without deep meaning.

Chapter 5

The "Do's and "Don'ts" of Shapership™: from MAD land to NO MAD land

Defining what Shapership™ means can be made easier by also defining what it "IS NOT".

For instance, Shapership™ is the Art of Shaping the Future and obviously not the Art of Preserving the Past. This is crucial in the current historical moment of disruption we are going through, because each of us has a choice to make: **Preserving the Old or Shaping the New.**

We believe it is impossible to operate with both **intentions** at the same time.

One pushes us to operate from the Past, trapped into the Regression Forces. The other is driven by our Desire to shape the New and help us operate from the Future, supported by the Opening Forces.

THE ART OF SHAPERSHIP

Insert 8: The choices to make: preserve the Old or Shape the New

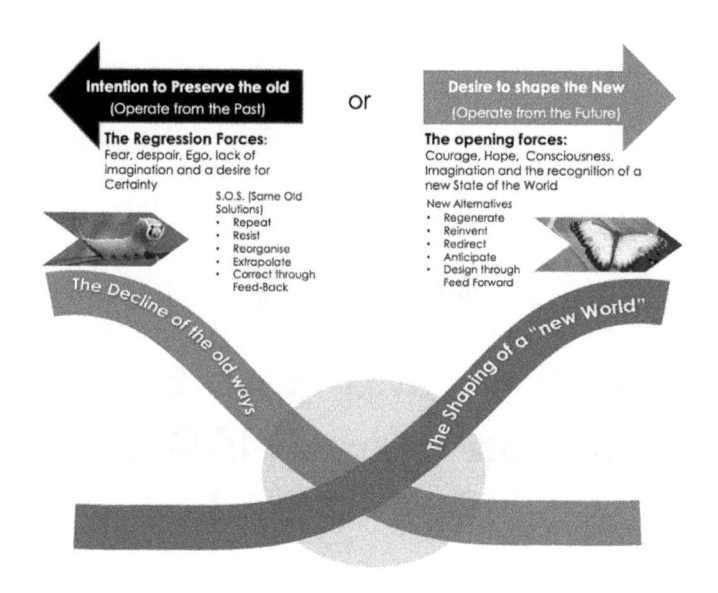

Intention to Preserve the old
(Operate from the Past)

or

Desire to shape the New
(Operate from the Future)

The Regression Forces:
Fear, despair, Ego, lack of imagination and a desire for Certainty

S.O.S. (Same Old Solutions)
- Repeat
- Resist
- Reorganise
- Extrapolate
- Correct through Feed-Back

The opening forces:
Courage, Hope, Consciousness, Imagination and the recognition of a new State of the World

New Alternatives
- Regenerate
- Reinvent
- Redirect
- Anticipate
- Design through Feed Forward

The Decline of the old ways

The Shaping of a "new World"

The metaphor of the metamorphosis from the caterpillar to the butterfly

It is really interesting to look at what is happening in the world right now.

The world out there seems to be going crazy. Whether we look at the Internet, read the newspapers or watch the TV news, we see there is a lot of upheaval going on around the planet.

What are we looking at? A world is collapsing while another is emerging right before our eyes.

It is the breakdown of an existing civilization and the simultaneous creation of a new thrivable Future.

All of this is happening right now for a simple reason: because our civilisation is destructive. Human civilisation has precipitated what is called the Sixth Mass Extinction of Life, we have undermined the web of Life so much that we cannot support ourselves in this world. We are going extinct, because of our behaviour.

We cannot build a sustainable civilisation on this foundation. Science says, we are facing a mass extinction, human civilisation has to recreate itself.

Confronted with all that, we can look at the situation in two very different ways.

Either locked into the Regression Forces – mainly Fear and Despair –promoted by the craziness we are experiencing, which then creates a worse situation because we get into protection "fences" and shut ourselves off.

Or we activate the Opening Forces and we recognise that what happens is right. It is the chaos of a Death process while a new state of the world is emerging.

A powerful metaphor might really help us see and understand what is happening in our world today as an opportunity: it is the metamorphosis of a caterpillar into a Butterfly. And this story actually replicates everything we are going through.

The caterpillar is a multicellular organization where all the cells are "individuals" working together in harmony in the caterpillar's body. But caterpillars are voracious organisms. When put on a plant, they will eat every leaf of that plant. They will destroy everything in their environment. Imagine a system made of 50 trillion cells, each one having a job - taking care of the breathing, the digestion, amongst others. - working hard all day and finding everything wonderful: the caterpillar is growing, it is getting bigger and bigger.

Then comes a point where the caterpillar reaches a certain size and stops destroying its environment.

It goes into a cocoon in which the metamorphosis process will ultimately create a Butterfly.

The difference is that the caterpillar is the most voracious of organisms and the butterfly has the lightest touch on Nature, perhaps it doesn't even touch the ground for most of its life.

Between the caterpillar and the butterfly, something is going on in that cocoon that relates to today's world.

In the early stages of the metamorphosis, the caterpillar undergoes a "breakdown" phase where the old structures begin to dissolve.

All of the sudden, things start to slow down. The caterpillar is no longer eating, nor moving, nor doing anything anymore. The cells are losing their job. They are doing nothing. There are no more jobs.

The body of the caterpillar starts to fall apart, and all these individual cells form a chaotic soup. Some of these cells are panicking because they look around and see that things are falling apart. To them, it seems to be "Apocalypse Now". In this state of fear, many cells actually commit suicide - which in Biology is called Apoptosis.

In that chaotic soup, while everybody is in panic and fear, other individual cells are not panicking at all. These are individual cells called "Imaginal Cells". They resonate on a different frequency. They have a different Vision of the Future. In the midst of this falling apart of their "civilization", they see that a more beautiful world is possible. They are the ones who create the Butterfly.

These Imaginal Cells are so different from other worm cells that the caterpillar's immune system, locked into its survival logic, mistakes them for enemies and uses vital energy to try to destroy them. From the caterpillar perspective, they are seen as a threat to the status quo. But more Imaginative Cells keep appearing.

The caterpillar's immune system can't destroy the Imaginal Cells fast enough.

Because of the system's breakdown, Imaginal cells start to form clusters called "imaginal grouping". These connection makes them stronger.

A tipping point is reached within the caterpillar.

The Imaginal Cells then guide the cells that are out of work, indicating there is a better civilization available. The Imaginal groupings are seen for what they are, prototyping the Future. Vital energy is used to nourish them rather than undermine them.

The metamorphic process unfolds. The cells that were breaking down from the caterpillar and the Imaginal Cells start to assemble into the new structure. They form a critical mass that recognizes their mission is to achieve the incredible birth of a Butterfly.

What is happening in the world today is the end of the caterpillar.

At this moment, Civilisation is in the metamorphosis stage of a voracious destructive civilization breaking down and the birth of a new viable civilization for the Future.

> *We are living in a time of thresholds being crossed and the more conscious we are of these shifts, the more able we are to help metamorphose our dominant logic.*
>
> *This fundamental and profound metamorphosis is nothing more, or nothing less than opening ourselves to who we naturally are."*[57]

---

[57] Gilles Hutchins, author of « the nature of Business. Designing for resilience » and « Future Fit

THE ART OF SHAPERSHIP

The Butterfly Civilisation

Part of the population is living the "end of the world". Without the capacity to imagine a new story, they are dominated by the old story that repeats itself eternally.

But, from the same population, which is experiencing the collapse of the caterpillar, "Imaginal Cells" are emerging and making themselves known with new ideas, new visions and new ways to escape the dying system. Because there is a better way out. It is not the end at all.

Those people have a new vision for the Future of this civilization. A Butterfly civilization which is far more magnificent, where we can thrive into the Future in community and harmony.

They say "Wait, we can restructure this thing. We can make something far better and radically different. We can build a new system that will make the previous one obsolete."

As Bruce Lipton, the great biologist says,

> *"Rather than looking at fear, right now, look at this as the moment of opportunity because there is something so much better on the Horizon, but we can only get there by eliminating the structure as it is now because this structure is provided for our extinction.*
>
> *So, it is not a bad thing that is happening. It is quite a wonderful thing that is happening. As long as you decide to be the imaginal cells rather than the cells that commit apoptosis.*
>
> *It is a choice.*
>
> *I can wear my citizen hat and go out there and go WWWWWHOOO, freaking myself out, interfere with my immune system with all the stresses. Or I can sit back and say, it*

is unfortunate, but it is necessary because without it, we will not evolve into the Future. We must build a better system at the expense of taking down the system that is causing the problem.

This is the most important step in the survival of the human civilisation. Rather than focusing on the caterpillar, the voracious organism that's dying, it is time for us to put our energy into the organism that is being born. That is the butterfly version of the Human civilization, where human have the lightest touch on the planet and can support our environment rather than undermining it.

Rather than focusing on the caterpillar, the voracious organism that is dying, we can put our energy into the Butterfly".[58]

It is not a matter for the caterpillar to become bigger and bigger.

What matters is to become a butterfly!

A deep transformation is needed.

Some might decide to fully commit to helping the butterfly to emerge. Some might decide to grow the caterpillar bigger and bigger or fight against the inevitable decline of the old ways, with the illusion that we will be "back" to a secure and known situation.

Whatever the decision, we must be aware that, through our attitudes, choices and actions, we have the collective power to shape our Future, individually and collectively.

---

[58] Bruce Lipton, the Butterfly analogy, https://youtu.be/bfwMtGVmYFY

THE ART OF SHAPERSHIP

Margaret Mead said, *"Never doubt that a small group of thoughtful, committed citizens can change the world; indeed, it's the only thing that ever has"*. [59]

The story of the metamorphosis can motivate us to fully participate, as "imaginal cells", as said in this insightful comment by Deepak Chopra: [60]

> *"I firmly believe, as do many others, that there is an evolutionary effervescence in the fabric of today's society. Despite the clamour of fear, greed, over-consumption and violence that is expressed through the social fabric, there is a union of men and women that we can call imaginative cells, which reveal a different world, a transformation, a metamorphosis.*
>
> *The Uruguayan poet Mario Benedetti wrote:* **"What would happen if one day we woke up and realized that we are the majority?"** *I claim that imaginative cells would dominate and bring out the butterfly from a world of verse. This is the time of awakening. Groups of imaginative cells are gathering everywhere; they are beginning to recognize each other; they are developing the organizational tools to increase the level of consciousness, so that the next stage of our human society will manifest itself, to create a new society that will cease to be a caterpillar and become a butterfly. A new dimension of Life, a more compassionate and just society, a humanity rooted in happiness and mutual understanding...Be enthusiastic cells!*

---

[59] Margaret Mead, anthropologist, recipient of the Planetary Citizen of the Year Award in 1978.

[60] Deepak Chopra (1946 -) is an Indian-American author and a world authority in vanguard alternative medicine approaches

*Connect with others, come together, gather...
and unite us all to build a New Humanity!"*

The Call to Wisdom

"Be careful about the Present you create because it must look like the Future you dream of".

This wisdom comes from a collective of women in Bolivia.

It is "Now o'clock!"

For each of us, "Now" is a historical moment, whether in Business and/or in Life, to raise good questions and make wise decisions.

We have a fundamental choice to make:

- lead wrong fights to preserve a **MAD** world leading to *Massive Assured Destruction*
- or foster right causes to imagine and shape a desirable **NO-MAD LAND** driven by *Mutually Assisted Development*. Grounded on new Values and worldviews, it might be the place for things we crave for such as Dignity, Beauty, Greatness, Nobility and Love

Despite legitimate fear and worry which may have trapped some of us in a horrible feeling of fatalisation or despair about the Future, this is the perfect moment to reconnect to something deep, meaningful, aspirational in each of us that has always been present but maybe dormant or kept silent: our "Soul Compass". The inner voice inside which knows this might be a good time to raise good questions, restore hopes and rewrite the story of our Life instead of trying to "repair" or "fix" the crisis.

Although many of us currently feel stuck by the external visible situation, we have to recognize our participation in this world. As Albert Einstein said, *"The world we have created is a product of our thinking"*. What we see above the surface is greatly created and maintained by our "worldviews", beliefs and models that are no longer fit for the Future.

We are not victims; we are co-creators.

Our "maps" create the Landscape.

Our "maps" are not the "landscape", but they define how we shape it.

MAD Land and NO MAD Land are two different "Landscapes" created and sustained by a set of completely different – and often unconscious "Maps" (worldviews, paradigms, beliefs, perceptions, stories and values).

So, viable and exciting Futures depend on our abilities to transform our mental maps. But we need to admit that we are like the prisoners of Plato's cave: we tend to mix our "ideas" with Reality. **Our maps are invisible to us.**

MAD Land and NO MAD Land made visible

This is why we have created a metaphorical Map which makes our mental Maps visible. It is a metaphor of two very different countries: MAD Land and NO MAD Land (with 9 areas and 348 metaphorical perspectives).

It can help us "redraw" our mental maps and adopt new points of view to shape a world we want more of.

It is a "Broadmap" and not a Roadmap.

Rather than telling how to move from A to B, this Broadmap enables to adopt **the Altitude Attitude**: a higher, global perspective.

It offers a "**helicopter**" view to any person who wants to get a broader view on an issue, a project or any other situation where "altitude" is key.

It enables to get out of "familiar" patterns and make better choices of direction.

Because, as Bertrand Picard, who went around the world in a balloon said: **"Direction comes from altitude".**

Here is a view of the outline of our Map.

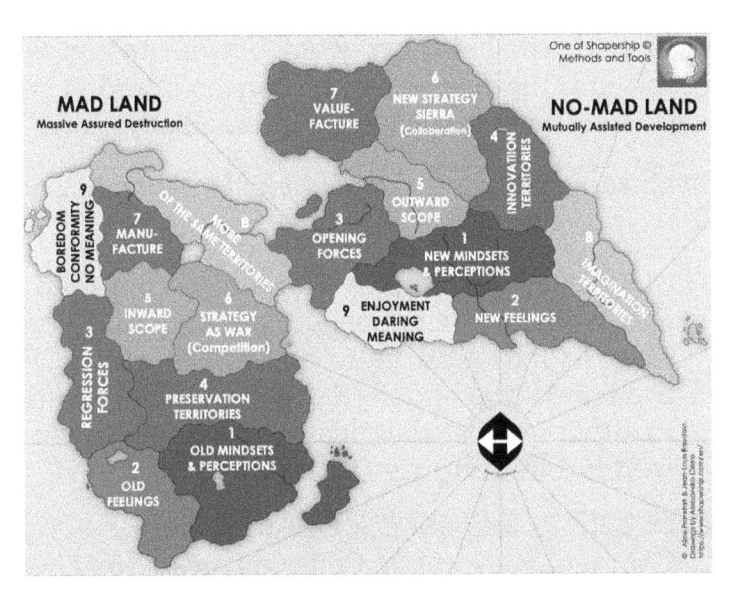

(We are currently preparing a book and a game based on it with a tentative title, "Broadmapping". You can see more details and visuals in color on our website, as well as a series of articles in our blog referring to specific captions. https://www.shapership.com/our-services/from-roadmapping-to-broadmapping)

As you can see, each of the 9 areas existing in Mad land has its "contrasted replica" in NO-Mad land.

THE ART OF SHAPERSHIP

	MAD LAND LEGENDS	NO-MAD LAND LEGENDS
1	Old Mindsets and Perceptions	New Mindsets and Perceptions
2	Old feelings (Fear, Deficiency needs, desire for Certainty)	New feelings (Courage, enthusiasm, Soul needs, readiness for Uncertainty)
3	Regression Forces: illusionary fights and lie to preserve the Status Quo)	Opening Forces (higher and issues - driven consciousness)
4	Preservation Territories	Innovation Territories
5	Inward Scope	Outward Scope
6	Strategy as War (Competition)	New Strategy Sierra (Collaboration)
7	Manufacture	Value-Facture
8	More of the same Territories	Imagination Territories
9	Boredom/Conformity/No meaning	Joy/Daring/Meaning

There is a logical build-up, from bottom to top which represents how the deepest levels (Zones 1, 2 and 3) impact the way we act or react and shape the visible world.

For instance, as citizens and professionals, depending on our Mindsets, perceptions and emotions, we can find ourselves

- captured by the **Regression** forces: confusion Fear, Ego, lack of imagination and a search for Certainty. They usually lead us to an inward-centric focus, Strategy as war and the S.O.S. (Same Old Solutions). In other words, they lead to **preserve the old instead of shaping the new.**

- or able to activate the **Opening** forces – Desire, Courage, Eco-centric Consciousness, Imagination – which will drive us to find new approaches to shape the Future.

First, let's take the "Altitude Attitude" to look at those "landscapes" and make the stories that support them visible.

MAD Land is an egocentric world of Materialism, driven by Rationalism, Left Brain, pseudo Lucidity and Realism "as an excuse for not trying".

It is

- focused on "Efficiency" (the Achievement age)

- based on Competition with others on whatever we perceive as scarce
- operating on Conformism and Comparison on "success", as defined in a dominant paradigm
- locked in "Incremental" Innovation to fix the problem, or Disruptive Innovation to make the same unsustainable things more efficiently
- driven by the Fear to lose or "lack"
- based on Clash, Exclusion, Power over (or passively waiting for leaders to create an alternative Future) and leading "wrong fights"

MAD land tends to be dominated by the story of "Scarcity" - a world of "not enough" - and by the "Machine paradigm", based on EGO needs and traditional "Leadership".

The story of Scarcity leads us to fight for the survival of the caterpillar - when renewal – the Butterfly - is what is actually needed.

NO MAD Land is a world of Integration: Cosmos-centric, driven by Soul needs, Inner Rightness, Whole Brain and Thinking Big for the World.

It is

- focused on serving the big issues of our time together (the Integral Age) thanks to Wisdom and Compassion
- based on (organic) Collaboration: the successful "we" in creating alternative Futures
- based on Imagination and an expanded view of what is possible (and what it means to be human)
- driven by "Transformative Visions" of a radically different Future and Transformative Innovation to create "alternative" stories based on Hope

- based on Dialogue, Inclusion, Power with others (Mayonnaise, Jazz), fighting together for the "Right Causes"

NO MAD Land is connected with a world of "Infinite Possibilities" and a story of Abundance based on Soul needs and Shapership™. It draws on our innate capacity to act according to our deepest Aspirations and Hopes, which is more than the satisfaction of our Needs or our Fear not to have enough.

The story of Abundance connects us with the cycle and flows of Life, which is in constant renewal. It helps us extend our perspectives and adopt "Butterfly Thinking": thinking and acknowledging birth and decline, accepting the falling of the leaf for the tree to regenerate itself. It guides us to participate in the transmutation of the caterpillar into a Butterfly.

It also connects us to more than what is "visible": the seeds of the Future, Imagination, Inspiration, Intuition, the places where "No Where" becomes "Now Here", a space where impossibilities become possibilities.

The paradigm is the Foe

Like fishes in the water, we take the paradigm in which we "swim" for granted. We don't see our lenses.

NO MAD Land is "nonvisible" by those using MAD land "lenses".

When we are trapped in the "MAD" cave – or "Iron Cage" as some people name it -, the known territory is what seems "normal". NO MAD Land appears as "illusionary".

To actively shape viable and exciting Futures in the long-term, we need a revolution in Minds.

New Thinking and new Mindsets to build a new world.

We have to get out of Plato's cave to realize that reality is a construction – and that we have the power and freedom to creatively and purposefully shift our perspectives, perceptions and beliefs to craft new realities.

To get out of the mess we're in, we need to create the **opposite of Fear; i.e. Desire.**

Now is the time to dare take a leap in Imagination to create counter-stories of the Future. **Meaning-Making stories** that resonate with our deepest aspirations, arouse Hope, Courage and Desire, the only forces capable of overcoming Fear, Despair, Violence and Regression.

Shapership™ is obviously an invitation to shift from MAD Land to NO MAD Land, from a worldview that limits our sense of possibilities to a radically different meaning-making story of the Future. One that includes our innate capacity, as human beings, to tell ourselves stories, to change those stories and to include our deepest Aspirations and Hopes into them. Because it makes sense.

It is an invitation to a shift in Identity, to change how we think and what we think.

THE ART OF SHAPERSHIP

From a high-level perspective, this is a shift.

From	To
· Being "stuck" in Problem saturated Stories, Dominant Worldviews, taken for granted ideas and beliefs	· Getting "Unstuck" with Preferred Meaning-Making stories, Alternative and Counter stories, Challenging approaches
· The Age of "Reason"	· The Age of "Unreason"[61]
· Orthodox approaches	· Unorthodox, subversive, imaginative approaches
· Conventional Wisdom	· Unconventional Wisdom
· S.O.S (Same Old Solutions) and Despair	· S.O.S (Save Our Souls) and Hope
· Known Territory (MAD land)	· Unknown Territory (NO MAD world)
· Doing More	· Un-doing

Shapership™ is an invitation to people of all ages who, **instead of focusing on repairing or fixing a dying MAD Land**, aspire to boost their Imagination, and actively shape a NO MAD Future for their family, communities, organizations, "territories" or field of practice.

---

[61] See note 9

New points of view to shape the Future everyday

Going into more details, we propose a short touristic visit to some points of interest in both MAD and NO MAD Lands.

Each location of the map metaphorically illustrates a point of view – not something we "are"; not something "good or bad" – but a way to look at the world and to shape it.

To make the visit more instructive, we have created a set of "mental cards", each of them associating two "contrasted" points of interest, one in MAD Land and the other in NO MAD Land. Each contrast provides us with **vantage points** from which we can, at the same time, observe the world we want less of and imagine the world we want more of.

Thanks to this reflective surface, we can also see how we participate in shaping the Future every day, either by maintaining the status quo, or by living the Future today.

We are invited to shift from a worldview that limits our sense of possibilities and keeps us stuck in the Present to a radically different meaning-making story of the Future.

The Left side is obviously dedicated to MAD land and the right side to NO MAD Land.

For instance, in the "Mindset and perceptions" area,

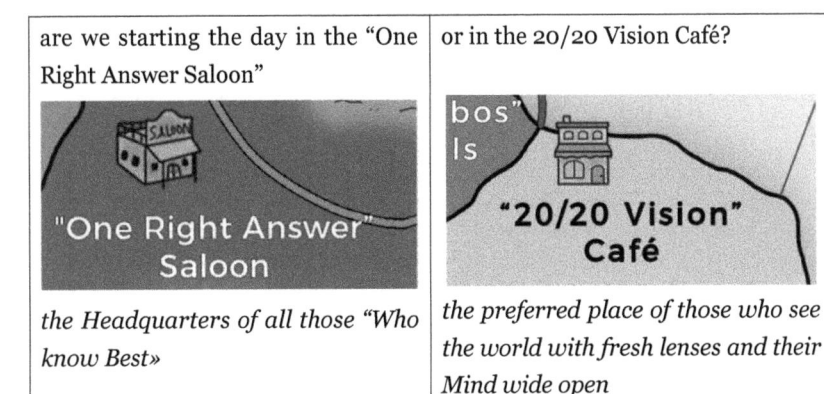

are we starting the day in the "One Right Answer Saloon"	or in the 20/20 Vision Café?
"One Right Answer" Saloon	"20/20 Vision" Café
the Headquarters of all those "Who know Best»	the preferred place of those who see the world with fresh lenses and their Mind wide open

THE ART OF SHAPERSHIP

Are we stuck into Rigid Rationalism based on the Past which leads us to the **"Realism Blind Spot"** 	Or do we see Reality as a realm of "infinite Possibilities", from **"Potentiality Springboard"?**
The limited perception of Reality "as it is" seen by people who lack Imagination and may nevertheless be at the top of organisations!	 *The area of Open Hearts and Minds which allows to have "Intuitions about what is possible, open new eyes, dream, dare Utopia". "I Believe, then I create".*
How can we get out from the **"Concrete jail"** in which we usually end up? 	The access is made possible thanks to **the "Vision to Action" Elevator**
The trap resulting from "Action without Vision". "I only believe what I see"	 *Where we connect Concepts and Ideas and understand that this is what really gives Power and Flexibility.*

ALINE FRANKFORT AND JEAN-LOUIS BAUDOIN

In this unpredictable world where there is much more unknows than knows, how can we make wise choices and move

from "**The Search for Certainty Shadows and Fog**" 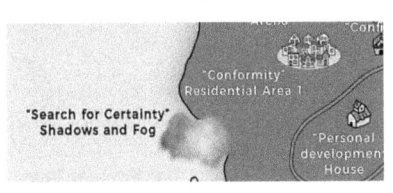	to the "**Confidence in Uncertainty Bay**"?
Here we feel as if we were wandering in the dark, by a foggy night, searching for an invisible friend who always vanishes, letting us completely **confused** by this disruptive and ambiguous situation. Trapped by our fear of "not knowing", our mind is locked into **Rigidity** and looks for places to maintain the **illusion** that things are under control, at least to a minimum.	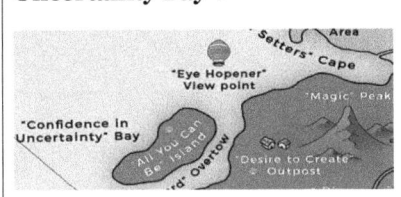 Where we abandon two of the biggest illusions of our times: the illusion of Control and of Predictability. We also give up our urge to have immediate concrete answers, open ourselves to more than one interpretation, imagine better Futures and start to experience the Confidence and Pleasure of navigating this **fuzzy** and **ambiguous** world.

Are we guided

by the "**Fear to Lose**" 	or by the "**Desire to Create**"? What can the consequences be?
Where our fears block any desire to contribute or any dream we may have	 Where we can hear the call to live a Life which makes a difference

THE ART OF SHAPERSHIP

Are we approaching

"**Strategy as War**", trying to be the best **in** the world? 	Or "**Strategy as Collaboration**", trying to be the best **for** the world? 
[map: "Strategy as War" Museum, "Arrogance" Tower, "Sameness" Arena, STRATEGY AS WAR (Competition), Competition Highway, "Shareho... Po...", "Industry & Markets" Limit, "Best in the World" Jungle]	*[map: Foundation, NEW STRATEGY SIERRA (Collaboration), Strate... Coopera..., "Abundance Valley", "Best for the World" Forum, "Collaboration" Interstate, "Economies of Scope" Congregation]*

How are we living our Life? Subjugated by the dominant ideas and worldviews of our time or driven by our search for a meaningful Life?

Conformity to a familiar MAD World often leads us to stick to the Known, even if it is meaningless and drives us to desperation 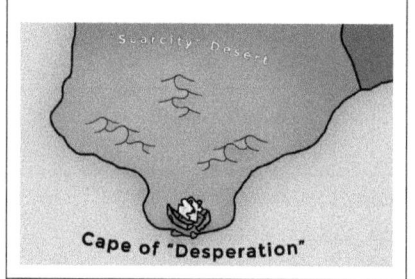	The Desire for a meaningful life drives our readiness to explore the unknow territory of NO MAD Land which is not visible yet but our "Soul compass" already knows is possible 
[map: Scarcity Desert, Cape of "Desperation"]	*[map: ...itheatre, "New Frontiers" Exchange, "Authenticity Cultural Center, "Shapership Peninsula", Cape of Hope]*
Every day, we take the **"Conforming" Road** *The predictable path that makes us act according to codes, rules and expectations we don't question nor disturb*	We travel on **"Daring" Lay Lines** *These lines enable us to tread on the Energy generated by something bigger than ourselves and that will enable us to reshape the World*

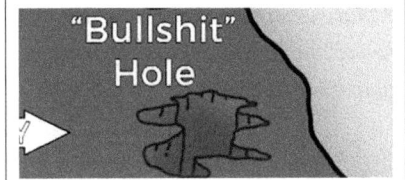

We are stuck in the **"Bullshit" Hole**	We especially like the **"No Bullshit" Freeway**
A hole that really stinks because of all the lies, bullshit jobs, meaningless statements and stupid strategies which have been thought and said all over the World. Some people have built their carrier on it!	*An authentic, scenic road to Simplicity and Authenticity, without useless signs and constraints*
We are lost in the "Denial" Fogs *Where we fall into the illusion that short-term corrective measures, standard and often repetitive solutions or logical adjustments will get us back to the status quo, even if it has become meaningless.* *But "It is not because the ostrich buries its head in the sand that you can't kick her butt."*	We live in **"Lucidity" Downtown areas** *Where we have the courage to see that, in order to create a meaningful Future, we can no longer reorganise the furniture in the same room. We need to reinvent the room. And in more and more instances, the building itself.*
We buy a house (that will take years to pay off) in **"Conformity" Residential Area** *Where it is deeply appreciated to respect Conventional Wisdom and Old Guard Ideas for generally accepted reasons such as "It is good for your career", "Her father is rich", etc*	We feel so good that everywhere is our **"All You Can Be" Island** *Where we dare to be all we can be, challenge Conventional Wisdom, look at the World with vanguard lenses and Paradigm-shifting Visions*

After years of conforming to other people's ideas we discover we are at **the "Carnival Masks" Museum**	Our favourite meeting place is **"Authenticity" Cultural Centre**
Here we find people who, after spending their Life masking who they really were, look like Lifeless wax dolls	*A place where we make room for ourselves and for others so we can all be genuinely ourselves*
We are driving full speed on **"Boredom" Highway**	We are traveling at our speed on **"In search of the Invisible" Highroad**
On this highway, Reality seems to be locked in the prison of Repetition, Banality, daily Routines, Meaninglessness. Every curve is similar to all the previous ones! Everything is so predictable that it is like the punchline of a joke that you already know: it is not funny	*On this winding road, we are ready for a wonderful inquiry and we direct our attention to uncover what might be a more interesting face of Reality: what is emerging and what is wanting to emerge. A surprise might be around the next curve, it challenge our reactions and our "driving" skills*

Do you want to continue?
So, let's go for another tour and feel the choices and preferences we might have for a point of view in MAD Land or in NO MAD Land (imagine a caption for each of those places)

In MAD Land, Society has accustomed us to use Thinking that is critical and judgment-based	**In NO MAD Land, we have learned Thinking that is constructive and creative**
We are lost in the **"Truth" Mirage**	We fill our mental tank at **"Proto-Truth" Station**
The illusion that the one and only Truth exists and that it will prove the others wrong	*Where we know there are only hypothesis and temporary perceptions of Truth*

We are stuck in **"the One Right Answer Saloon"**, *the Headquarters of all those "Who know Best"*	We can be nurtured by many good questions and answers in **the "20/20 Vision Café"**, *the preferred place of those who see the world with fresh lenses and their Mind wide open*
We frequently hit **the "A Priori" Wall** *Where we hear ourselves say (or think): "Don't bother me with facts, my mind is already made up!"*	This is close to the **"A Priori Reflection" Pool** *Where Fluidity is added to what could otherwise be rigidified*
This area is visited for its famous **"Rock Logic" Monument** *A monument erected to the Logic of Opposition, Adversarial Thinking, Exclusion, Fight to Win and Destruction*	It leads to **"Water Logic" Estuary** *Symbol of Parallel Thinking, the Path of Least Resistance follows the flow of Life.* *Like water, Life always wins!*
One place whose impact is largely underestimated in MAD Land is the **"Intelligence" Trap** *This is where people who think they are intelligent - and therefore think they think well - fall. They often move fast, through pseudo-logical reasoning, from wrong premises to wrong conclusions*	One of the most precious area in NO MAD land is the **"Think2Think" Archipelago** *A place where we have a capacity to think about the way we think, reflect about our own perceptions and hypothesis, connect and integrate various points of views, act with a Vision, keeping a helicopter view in tune with Reality. This is part of the Altitude Attitude.*

THE ART OF SHAPERSHIP

And no doubt, one of the sacred places of the land is the **"Idea Killer" Shrine** The place where any good and new idea risks to be murdered by so-called "normal" people who enjoy the easy satisfaction of killing ideas rather than proposing new ones. *Possibilities are turned into impossibilities.*	What helps us are **New "Concepts Nests"** *Safe places to give birth to disruptive concepts and ideas because we recognize them as seeds of the Future, as the potential of thousands of fruits.* *Impossibilities become possibilities.*
We are risking our Life and our Future at **"Critical Spirit" Gorge** *The narrow passage from which some people can look only at the reasons to destroy any project, idea or proposal in the shortest possible time.* *It probably satisfies their EGO, even gives them the illusion of defending the Truth, yet it is the best shortcut to status quo.* *By the way, it is always easier to criticize a chair than to design a new one*	An immense satisfaction comes from visiting **"Alternatives" Gold Mines** *Alternatives are the "nuggets" of today and tomorrow. Once extracted, washed, polished and honed, they demonstrate we are not imprisoned into the "one and only way to do" and that we can live in a world of infinite possibilities.* *Alternatives Gold Mines are places where we co-create meaningful Futures, new approaches to Wealth-creation which embody our Aspirations and Hopes*
We don't even understand Creativity very well and fall into the **"Crazitivity" Lake** *Where people locked in old perceptions have the illusion that freely expressing anything that goes through their mind will generate valuable concepts and ideas*	Since we are serious about the Value of Creativity, we have a **"Serious Creativity" Domain** *Where Creativity is the capacity to generate real and pertinent Value within well-identified constraints, through liberating structures*

MAD Land is where things are taken for granted"	NO MAD land is where the familiar is made "exotic"
We find ourselves stuck into the **"Small Thinking" Cave** *Where we slowly die, in the prison of facts and appearances*	Getting out of the cave of dominant "representations", we reach the **"Big Thinking" Clearing** *Where we adopt new lenses, dare challenge and Imagine how to think big and "radical" about ourselves and about how we want to participate in the transformation of the world, for ourselves, our communities and Society, in ways that generate Hope that viable Futures are possible.*
We are sinking into **"Assumptions" Swamps** *Where we are paralysed by the "dominant" ideas, perceptions, stories and beliefs we take for granted without challenging them or "resisting"*	The "Altitude Attitude" makes us discover **Constant Challenge Peak** *Far away from the «Comfort Zone», this is where we creatively deconstruct and reconstruct our Reality*
Lack of Imagination is often due to frequent visits to **"Blindness" Falls** *Where all we can see is nothing else than the familiar and the known... and we keep believing this is all there is to see.* *N.B. We will probably never see any black swan because we don't believe they exist!*	We start your journey at **"Curiosity" Harbour** *Where we look around and discover what is happening out there. It might be different than what we thought... Who knows? There might even be grey swans!*

THE ART OF SHAPERSHIP

It leads to **"Repetition" Swamps** *Where we are busy downloading the same habits of thoughts, leading to endless reproduction of "more of the same", which, we believe, is Thinking!*	Then, we move on to **"Imagination" Range** *Where Imagination and Audacity enable us to discover new landscapes, to give voice to what wants to emerge, including Hopes and Aspirations, to envision possible Futures even though the present situation may be far removed from that possibility*
We are locked in the **"Nine Points" Roundabout** *Where we remain imprisoned by our daily Thinking routines and try to solve problems using the same Thinking that created them*	We reach the **"New Frontiers" Exchange** *Where we shift our perspectives, adopt new worldviews and discover more attractive alternative roads to move forward*

We are victims of what Einstein called the "biggest illusion of our time: Separation"	**We enter into a world on "inter-being" and Oneness**
We wander in **Fragmented views Forest** *Where we see the parts and take them for the whole -our Thinking is based on Disconnection, Categories, Competition, Me versus Them - turning today's solutions into tomorrow's problems.*	We step back and look at the **Big Picture Panorama** *Where we expand our awareness of the changing context, allowing us "Holism with focus" - see the parts and the whole - sense the connections and the flows, move to Communityship and Collaboration*

Our Thinking comes from the **"Or" School** *Where occidental people are taught to put the "real world" into "boxes", where each thing is classified in its own category, inherited from the Past, separated from the rest.* *Friends or enemies. Innocent or Guilty. Black or White. Partners or Competitors. Food Industry or Health...*	We are educated in the **"And" School** *Where we learn that most categories and boundaries only exist in our minds, that it is useful to dissociate and to integrate. Connecting with an "AND" brings more Value in the real World.* *1+1 = 2, when there is a +.* *Food + Energy + Mobility + Health....*
In this territory, we also find the usual Separation between Mind, Body and Soul, with a dominating mental; this is the **"Heads and Hands Split"** *Where those who "Think" are separated from those who "Do". That generates "Bullshit Vision Statements" and abstract strategies, in line with "mental maps" of what should happen, but detached from Reality*	We can visit **"Head and Hands Tango" Circle** *Where we "tango" with Reality.* *Connecting Body, Mind, Soul, we have a helicopter view - yet not detached from Reality. We are in tune with the World. We sense tensions from the field, let ourselves be informed and adapted by the grounded Reality of what is needed and being called for the World. We can jump into the Unknown, without Anxiety and ready to "act" with a Vision, open to Intuition and Inspiration*

THE ART OF SHAPERSHIP

In MAD Land, we are used to Thinking that emphasises Analysis of the Known.	In NO MAD Land, we practice Thinking that emphasis exploration of the Unknown, Movement and expanded Perspectives
Our Rigid Rationalism often leads us to compromise and dull Thinking, as valued in the **"Tradition" Temple** *Where Tradition is erected to a sort of Religion and used to justify attacks and criticisms on Novelty and Differences, from a "righteous" posture*	We adhere to the **"Positive Revolution" Community** *Where the desire to generate a Creative Transformation and to move forward for the benefit of the many, generates Design, Development and good Humour*
We are familiar with the **"Linear logic Road"** *that leads straight from A to B, without making any side roads visible* It usually ends at the **"Quick Conclusion" Stop** *The point where we jump to, far too early, and stop Thinking, obsessed by the need to find the "one right answer" ...ASAP!*	We love the **"System View" Terrace,** *where we visualize the system of connectedness we are embedded in* This allows us to visit **"In-Depth Thinking" Fields** *to make wiser decisions and build the Future on conscious choices*

The Conformity to a familiar MAD World often leads us to stick to the Known, even if it is meaningless	The Desire for a meaningful life drives our readiness to explore the unknow territory of NO MAD Land which is not visible yet but our "Soul compass" already knows is possible
Every day, we take **the "Conforming" Road** *The predictable path that makes us act according to codes, rules and expectations we don't question nor disturb*	We travel on **"Daring" Lay Lines** *These lines enable us to tread on the Energy generated by something bigger than ourselves and that will enable us to reshape the World*

We are stuck in the **"Bullshit" Hole** *A hole that really stinks because of all the lies, bullshit jobs, meaningless statements and stupid strategies which have been thought and said all over the World. Some people have built their carrier on it!*	We especially like the **"No Bullshit" Freeway** *An authentic, scenic road to Simplicity and Authenticity, without useless signs and constraints*
We are lost in the "Denial" Fogs *Where we fall into the illusion that short-term corrective measures, standard and often repetitive solutions or logical adjustments will get us back to the status quo, even if it has become meaningless.*	We live in **"Lucidity" Downtown areas** *Where we have the courage to see that, in order to create a meaningful Future, we can no longer reorganise the furniture in the same room. We need to reinvent the room. And in more and more instances, the building itself.*
We buy a house (that will take years to pay off) in **"Conformity" Residential Area** *Where it is deeply appreciated to respect Conventional Wisdom and Old Guard Ideas for generally accepted reasons such as "It is good for your career", "Her father is rich", etc*	We feel so good that everywhere is our **"All You Can Be" Island** *Where we dare to be all we can be, challenge Conventional Wisdom, look at the World with vanguard lenses and Paradigm-shifting Visions*
After years of conforming to other people's ideas we discover we are at **the "Carnival Masks" Museum** *Here we find people who, after spending their Life masking who they really were, look like Lifeless wax dolls*	Our favourite meeting place is **"Authenticity" Cultural Centre** *A place where we make room for ourselves and for others so we can all be genuinely ourselves*

We are driving full speed on **"Boredom" Highway**	We are traveling at our speed on **"In search of the Invisible" Highroad**
On this highway, Reality seems to be locked in the prison of Repetition, Banality, daily Routines, Meaninglessness. Every curve is similar to all the previous ones! Everything is so predictable that it is like the punchline of a joke that you already know: it is not funny	*On this winding road, we are ready for a wonderful inquiry and we direct our attention to uncover what might be a more interesting face of Reality: what is emerging and what is wanting to emerge. A surprise might be around the next curve, it challenges our reactions and our "driving" skills*

Fear is the worst guide we can imagine but it develops its strategies to lock us down in MAD Land	**Desire is opening our connection to Life and a new spirit blows everywhere**
One of its most frequent strategies is to invade us with a representation of a Future we don't want; **the "Fear to Lose" Theatre of the Mind** *The stage where we see the Future as a threat to what we have acquired, and our Vision is driven by Fear*	We find it in the **"Life-Affirming Purpose" Amphitheatre** *The place where we trust the plot and develop the confidence that moving on with the flow of Life will bring the world Happiness and new possibilities*
At every crossroad, we see a **"Fear to Lose" Station** *Where our fears block any desire to contribute or any dream we may pursue*	We multiply visits to the **"Desire to Create" Outpost** *Where we can hear the call to live a Life which makes a difference*
We move up the "Fear" Tower *Where all Fears, that we don't even dare to face anymore – and generally disguise under good logical "reasons" -, prevent us from leaving what we know for the "scary" Unknown*	Despite our fear, we can decide to take the **"Courage" Causeway** *The magnificent road that awaits those who have moved beyond their fears and can begin to admire the new landscapes of Freedom*

And of course, because fear is a self-fulfilling prophecy, our fear of lacking creates its Reality. We live in **"Scarcity" Desert** *Here, we are dominated by the story of "not enough", always looking for "more" to satisfy our needs and driven by the fear not to satisfy them.* *We fight for the "Survival of the Caterpillar", when it is Renewal – the Butterfly – that is needed!*	Our choices are driven by our Inner Rightness, in the **"Abundance" Forest** *Where we live in a world of "Infinite Possibilities", with a story of Abundance and constant renewal, drawing on our innate capacity to act according to our deepest aspirations and hopes. We adopt "Butterfly" Thinking: i.e. we participate in the transmutation, we die to our old mental representations, giving birth to a new state of Consciousness and to a new world*
The search for Certainty, Control and Predictability leads us to abhor the VUCA era: Volatility, Uncertainty, Complexity and Ambiguity	**We are ready to "accept" Life as it is and put Wisdom at work in VUCA times revisited: Velocity, Unorthodoxy, Creativity and Awesomeness[62]**
We pay daily visit to the **"Desire for Certainty" Abbey** *Where we pray to obtain some reliable reasons to move on because we are completely confused by this disruptive and ambiguous world. We feel as if we were wandering in the dark, by a foggy night. Trapped by our fear of not knowing, our mind is locked into Rigidity and looks for places to maintain the illusion that things are, at least to a minimum, under control*	We surf on the waves of the **"Confidence in Uncertainty" Bay** *Where we abandon two of the biggest illusions of our time: the illusion of Control and of Predictability. We also give up our urge to have immediate concrete answers, open ourselves to more than one interpretation, imagine better Futures and start to experience Confidence and Pleasure in navigating this fuzzy and ambiguous world*

---

[62] Thanks to the Futurist Gerd Leonard for his new interpretation of VUCA

We are a full member of **the "Confirm-The-known" club** *Where what we call Thinking is mainly downloading, recognizing and confirming what we know*	We happily belong to the **"Explore the Unknown" Network** *Where we dare to acknowledge the difference between what we thought and what we discover, reflect on it and venture into the Unknown*
Our Life is stuck in **the "Comfort" Zone** *Where our decisions are motivated by our inner need to stick to what we know*	We know **the "Magic" Peak** *Where our decisions are motivated by our desire to explore the Unknown, to free ourselves from useless conditionings and to open new paths towards a meaningful Life*
We don't escape **the "Do" stuffy house** *This is a place filled with people keeping themselves super "busy" with all the things they do, all the stuff they have, because the issue is to keep busy without questioning the meaning of it. They are in Hell, in the pursuit doing more and faster*	Every day, we visit the **"Undo" Contemplation Space** *This is the vital space for doing nothing, change gears, undo, take time to contemplate, find Inspiration, think, and revisit what we do to do the right things*

We use the real world as an excuse, we fall into Disillusion, Fatalisation and Despair, Powerlessness, Demotivation and Meaninglessness	We commit to make this world a better place, despite everything. We want to reinvent and re-enchant the world beyond Money, to bring out a new paradigm, a renewed sense of Possibility, Meaning making and "Passion
We are drawn into **the "Backward" (Regression) Undertow**	We move with the **"Forward" Over tow**
Where we engage into illusionary fights, denials and lies, combined in a backward "tide" designed to preserve the Known: The Comfort Zone, the Profit Zone, the Power Zone, the Control Zone, even the "Rage Zone"	*Where we are ready for the recognition of a new state of the World and engage in active participation to the forward-oriented Movement with Imagination, Intelligence, Courage and Purpose (Faith)*
We are dominated by **"Fatalisation" Viewpoint**	We decide to go to **"Hope" Power Station**
Where what happens is seen as "fate" against which nothing can be done. And nothing will be done	*A place where we can start imagining better Futures which generate possibilities of Change and Meaning*
No return is possible from **"Despair" Islands**	This is a leap we need to make to **"Faith" City**
A place where we are desperate about "the way things are", persuaded we are powerless when confronted with Power and Paradigms, that we are "locked" in "more of the same" or "worse". The type of mindset that makes us think it is useless to try anything anyway!	*A place where we make a leap in Faith, not because we have evidences that things are moving forward in a "good direction," but because we have decided to trust the innate capacity of human beings to act according to their deepest aspirations and hopes to DO GOOD*

THE ART OF SHAPERSHIP

We sink into **"Powerlessness" Lake** with a feeling of Helplessness, Powerlessness and Depression, in relation with the old games, with the dominant Powers and Paradigms which fight so well to stay in power	We enjoy the **"Power-with" Pool** A place to find Hope and Optimism. We can change the world. We don't need to have a title or hold a position to make an impact. We can rally a formidable ecosystem of actors to generate transformative Action

Trapped in our Ego-centric logic, we have a loan mower perspective.	**We are practicing the Altitude Attitude, move to an ECO system Perspective**
We find No way out of **"Ego Centric" Canyon** Where our Vision is narrowed by the little "Me, I and Myself, focused on "what I desire"	We take the trip to **"Eco Centric" Panorama** Here we open ourselves beyond "mental" dimensions to" something Bigger than ourselves, what is desirable for the world, our contribution to the Community and the issues of our time"
We live behind "Ego Protection" fences Where we are so vulnerable that we stand behind rigid protection fences which are invisible to us but might seem imposing or aggressive from outside	**We are searching the "Ego dissolution" area** `Where we enjoy living and sharing authentically, feeling no need to maintain appearances and knowing that Vulnerability is our strongest human charm
We live in "Ego" Tower Where our choices, even when we make strategic decisions impacting thousands of people, are dominated by the satisfaction of Deficiency needs: fear of failure, fear of not being loved, insecurity, need for power or status	**We create an internal "Soul" Bridge** What connects us to broader aspirations of our Soul to make a difference, contribute to the Beauty, the Dignity, the Nobility of Life

From Capitalism Realism to Hope and Wisdom: Choosing our preferred Future

In his last book, "Beyond Survival. Practical Hope in Powerful Times", Graham Leicester writes

> *"Raymond Williams tells us that our task is "to make hope possible rather than despair convincing". But for me hope is always possible. The real challenge at this point is to make it convincing. Then it might attract the resources to match our ambitions and, just as 'lockdown' has proved a more or less global immediate response to the pandemic, hope might frame for everyone the invigorating spirit of the next phase – recovery and renewal. Despair is more alluring. 'The devil always has the best tunes.' The hopeful story, by contrast, touches a precious place in us and is more demanding of the listener. It is easier to dismiss visionary alternatives as unrealistic and utopian than to acknowledge, as Cecil Collins suggests in the epigraph above, that their very imagining represents a challenge to who we are, what we regard as living, and what we are prepared to stand for today."*[63]

We (Aline and Jean-Louis) adopt the hypothesis made by modern Science that the Future already exists as a potential, i.e. that all the possibilities exist but only some of them will come to materialize and become Reality.

Now more than ever, we need to imagine the possibility of a viable Transformation, and intentionally commit to make this preferred Future happen.

---

[63] Beyond Survival. Practical Hope in powerful times, Graham Leicester, Triarchy Press, 2020

> *"Primarily, everybody lives in the future because they strive.*
> *Past things only come later, and as yet genuine present is almost never there at all. The Future dimension contains what is feared or what is hoped for. As regards human intentions, that is, when it's not thwarted, it contains only what is hoped for. (...)*
> *Function and content of hope are experienced continuously and in times of rising societies, they have been continuously activated and extended.*
> *Only in times of a declining old society, like modern western society, does a certain partial and transitory intention run exclusively downwards. Then those who cannot find their way out of the decline, are confronted with fear of hope and against it.*
> *Then fear presents itself as the subjectivist nihilism, as the objective masks of the crisis phenomenon, which is tolerated but not seen through, which is lamented but not changed."*[64]

If stories shape our Lives, let's change our stories.

We have the power to change our own Reality

- by being **aware** of those stories

- by being **free** to challenge and **escape** those we don't want

- by using the power of our **imagination to make alternative** stories **EMERGE**

- by **weaving** new relationship with the Future, we **desire** for ourselves and our Society

---
[64] The Principle of Hope: v.1 (studies in contemporary German social thought), Ernst Bloch

- by making **conscious** and wise choices based on freer and expanded perspectives.

Since the Future is unpredictable, then why not choose the one we desire?

Each of us can imagine alternative Futures and put an intention on the one we wish to see materialize one day.

By doing that, we create the Memory of the Future.

And then we can turn this potential into Reality.

EM-BODY it.

Each one of us can boost its Imagination and contribute to the emergence of a "Story of the Future" interwoven with his/her Hopes, Desires and Aspirations.

This new map will shape the landscape.

It will help the metamorphosis from the caterpillar into the Butterfly.

And if we collectively adopt "Butterfly Thinking", we can really change the world.

Hope might be the best path forward.

It is the counter-story of everything which maintains us "stuck" into the "Regression Forces" (Fear, Denial, Despair, Resignation and Cynicism).

Exactly like "creating" is resisting Stupidity, Imagination is resisting the "impossibility of Change", Hope is resisting Hopelessness, one of the most insupportable things, downright intolerable to human needs.

> "Who are we? Where do we come from? Where are we going? What are we waiting for? What awaits us? Many only feel confused. The ground shakes and they don't know why

> *and what to do. There is a state of anxiety. If it becomes more definite, then it is fear. (...)*
> *It is a question of learning Hope.*
> *Its work does not renounce.*
> *It is in love with success rather than failure. Hope, superior to fear is neither passive nor locked into nothingness.*
> *The emotion of hope goes out of itself, makes people broad instead of confining them, cannot know enough of what it is that makes them inwardly aimed, of what may be allied to them outwardly.*
> *The work of that emotion requires people to throw themselves actively in what is becoming, to which they themselves belong.*
> *It will not tolerate a dog's life which feels itself only passively thrown into what is, which is not seen through, even wretchedly recognized.[65]"*

Hope is a choice to believe that the Future is a world of becomingness, that there is still an undisclosed space of indeterminacy in front of us and that the destiny of man is not nothingness. It is a faith that we can ultimately orient ourselves in the rising horizon of our consciousness, towards the royal road through the realm of possibilities that also leads to what is critically needed.

It is also taking a stand, participating in taking things as they are and as they go, therefore as they could go radically better.

Because it makes sense.

> *"Hope is a dimension of the Soul*
> *And not an objective assessment of a situation*

---

[65] The Principle of Hope: v.1 (studies in contemporary German social thought), Ernst Bloch

Hope is not the conviction that something will turn out well but the certainty that something makes sense, regardless of how it turns out."[66]

The "Do's and "Don'ts" of Shapership™

In this part, we illustrate what Shapers DO and DO NOT DO to shape the Future.

Beyond their actions, we make an attempt to clarify the Attention and Intentions from which they see, think and act.

Intentions are sustained by our "Soul Compass" which goes very deep under the surface. They give a precise orientation to our actions and, just as it is physically impossible to go simultaneously in opposed directions, some intentions are impossible to pursue at the same time.

Preserving the caterpillar – which pushes us to operate from the Past – is opposite to fighting for the birth of the Butterfly – which leads us to operate from the Future.

---

[66] Vaclav Havel, Meditation on Hope

THE ART OF SHAPERSHIP

Shapership™ is an inside-out process. It is based on "Shifts in Minds for Shifts in Action"[67].

Operating from the Past is what we call being locked in the **Regression Forces**, with a gamut of visible "symptoms"

- Repeat
- Repair
- Reorganize
- Extrapolate
- Correct through feed back

Operating from the Future is being driven by the **Opening forces** which manifest through visible "behaviours"

- Regenerate
- Reinvent
- Redirect
- Anticipate
- Design through feed-Forward

The "Don'ts" of Shapership™ Operating from the Past	The "Do's" of Shapership™ Operating from the Future
1. Shapers don't necessarily "HOLD" a position "at the top" of anything.	1. Shapers "ARE" the Change they want to see happen. Who they are and what they do often initiates a "Movement". They are "History Makers"
2. Shapers don't want to **PRESERVE** the Past - the Comfort zone, the Profit Zone, the Power Zone, the Control Zone, etc.	2. They want to generate a **CREATIVE TRANSFORMATION** and initiate a positive "Revolution" to the benefit of the many, way beyond their self-interest. They want to move toward a more just, inclusive and sustainable Future

---

[67] Creative ConsulTeam's (the authors' company's Baseline)

3. Shapers don't engage in a **BACKWARD** movement: illusionary fights, denials and lies to preserve the status quo, eliminate "symptoms", "escape" Reality and get back to the "known situations"	3. Shapers catalyse a **FORWARD** Movement which starts with the recognition of a new state of the world and a commitment to participate to this emerging Future with Imagination, Intelligence, Courage and Purpose
4. Shapers don't lead **WRONG FIGHTS** like focusing on "Having", on "Profit Maximization", etc., which lead to **M**utually **A**ssured **D**estruction (MAD)	4. They defend **RIGHT CAUSES**; they want a **NO** MAD World based on their version of MAD: **M**utually **A**ssured **D**evelopment. A more just, inclusive and sustainable Future
5. Shapers don't resist or react to Novelty with a **"BUSINESS AS USUAL" ATTITUDE**	5. They are committed to create Novelty. Whatever the field, they pioneer **"BUSINESS AS UNUSUAL"**, "Life as Unusual", "Law as unusual", "Philosophy as Unusual", etc.
6. Shapers don't **CONFORM** to obsolete ideas or conventional Wisdom with usual pretexts. They don't refuse to venture into the "Unknown" for commonly accepted "reasons" such as "We don't know", "There is more to lose than to gain", "There is no certainty" which characterizes old guard or self-centred individuals	6. Shapers **DARE** "the Age of Unreason" [68] when it leads to greater "Wisdom". They have PARADIGM-SHIFTING VISIONS, they look at the World with vanguard "lenses", they challenge conventional Wisdom

---

[68] Charles Handy, "The Age of Unreason"

7. Shapers don't use **REALITY AS AN "EXCUSE"** for not trying, making it a prison for Repetition. As Jason Fried & David Heinemeir Hansson brilliantly put it in their book "Rework" [69]: *"The real world isn't a place, it's an excuse. It's a justification for not trying"*.	7. Shapers have their way to **FACE and SEE Reality as it is and as it is becoming.** They are not "prisoners" of appearances. They have an "intuition of what is possible", they know that *"what could be is richer than what is"*. [70] They recognize an emerging state of the world is needed and engage in authentic questioning, no "bullshit" talk, participation to the movement with Imagination, Intelligence, Audacity, and Purpose
8. Shapers are not driven by **FEAR, EGO** or a desire for **CERTAINTY which maintains people in Known territories**	8. They are driven by **Courage**, Enthusiasm, long-term **Aspirations** beyond themselves and a readiness to navigate **UNCERTAINTY and explore Unknown territories**

---

[69] Rework, Jason Fried & David Heinemeir Hansson, Crow Business, ISBN 978-0-307-46374-6

[70] Henry Bergson

9. Shapers don't write motorcycle user manuals without knowing what a motorcycle is. They refuse **the OLD SEPARATION between Vision and Action,** Mind and Matter, Head and Hands which generates "Bullshit Statement" or Visions and abstract strategies, in line with "mental maps" of what should happen but detached from Reality. They don't' write "**RIGID** plans" in which extrapolated data helps explain the Future, giving the illusion of control but toothless in the face of unpredictable forces operating in the world outside

9. Shapers have "***The Altitude Attitude***". They have a helicopter view - **yet NOT DETACHED from Reality or the "material" at hand.** They "tango" with Reality and are **IN TUNE** with the world. **CONNECTING** Body +Mind and Soul, they see, sense act, guided by the grounded Reality of what is being called for in the world and by their inner "soul compass", which knows "what needs to be done". This gives them a direction, a meaningful purpose larger than themselves, guiding rules and strategies which are in harmony with "Reality" and its fundamental Uncertainty. They jump into the unknown, "acting" with a Vision. Their strategies, organizations and approaches are semi-coherent, emergent, adaptive, agile, responding to a world they also take part in creating. They know *"No one can predict the Future. All we can do is choose our contribution to the circumstances out of which the Future will take its shape."* [71]

---

[71] The Age of Heretics: Heroes, Outlaws and the Forerunners of Corporate Change *by* Art Kleiner

10. Shapers don't change people	10. They change the way people "see". They expand people's Vision of what is possible, of what they can do and of who they can become
11. Shapers don't focus on **CONTROL**; they have abandoned the illusion that it is possible anyway	11. They balance **FOCUS and FREEDOM**. They lead from within and they connect everyone beyond boundaries - organizational and others- to create Collective Action and solve real issues. They act with others for this larger Purpose they allow to unfold, they listen and see with Openness, Empathy and a broadened Consciousness to generate a movement based on co-creation. There is no Mind/Matter, no Thinker/Doer split
12. When they are "chosen" as Leaders, Shapers don't "EMPOWER" others because Empowerment supposes somebody has the Power to empower others who don't have the Power	12. They SHARE Power to foster transformative Dialogue and Action
13. Shapers don't always have titles	13. They always have personal Authority
14. Shapers are not **Undertakers**, their vocation is not to bury companies, generating their own income from Death and Sorrow	14. They are **Over-givers**, serving intelligent and value-creating initiatives that generate beneficial outcomes for the entire system

Insert 8: the "Do's" and "Don'ts" of Shapership™

The Do's and Don'ts of Shapership

The Don'ts of Shapership Operating from the Past	The Do's of Shapership Operating from the Future
The Regression Forces Repeat Resist Reorganise Extrapolate Correct through feed back	The Opening Forces Regenerate Reinvent Redirect Anticipate Design through feed-Forward

1. Holding a position
2. PRESERVATION of the Past
3. BACKWARD Movement: Illusionary fights, denials and lies to preserve the status quo, eliminate "symptoms" and be back to known situations ("Comfort Zone")
4. WRONG FIGHTS (focus on Having, profit maximisation, etc.) which leads to MAD: Mutually Assured Destruction
5. Business as USUAL: Resistance to Change and Novelty, Fear to lose, focus on "Value for Money"
6. CONFORMING to Conventional Wisdom and old guard ideas with usual pretexts
7. Taking reality as an "EXCUSE" for not trying, making it a prison for repetition
8. Driven by Fear, Ego or Desire for Certainty
9. Old SEPARATION between Vision and Action, disconnected Body, Mind and Soul: abstract and mental Visions and strategies detached from Reality, making rigid "plans"
10. Changing people
11. Focusing on control
12. My status, Empowering others
13. Undertakers

1. Being the change
2. Creative TRANSFORMATION and positive revolution to shape the Future
3. FORWARD movement: recognition of a new state of the World and participation to the Movement with Imagination, Intelligence, Courage and Purpose
4. RIGHT CAUSES which lead to a NO Mad world and a new version of MAD: Mutually Assured Development
5. Business as UNUSUAL: Enthusiasm, Courage to challenge and Commitment to the creation of new realities, Focus on "Value for Many"
6. DARING the "Age of Unreason", vanguard lenses and paradigm shifting visions
7. Facing and SEEING Reality as it is and as it is becoming, without being prisoners of appearances, with authenticity, no Bullshit
8. Driven by Courage, Enthusiasm, Aspirations beyond themselves and readiness to navigate Uncertainty
9. Acting with a Vision, CONNECTING levels, Helicopter view in tune with the world, guiding rules and agile approaches
10. Changing the way people see
11. Balancing Focus and Freedom
12. Authority, sharing Power, creating a Movement
13. Over-Givers

Chapter 6

Shapership™ put in action by some impressive People

Here is the subjective choice of Shapers we made to illustrate our concept.

As we said earlier, although their road is often paved with obstacles and difficulties, their Life may be a source of inspiration.

Maria Montessori (Italy 1870-1952) - Shaper of a new approach to Education

Maria Montessori has been one of the most innovative Childhood pedagogues of the 20th Century. She initiated a worldwide movement in Education.

1. Creative Resistance: The Big "NO".

> Maria Montessori graduates from the University of Rome in 1896 as Italy's first woman Doctor in Medicine, at a time when women were not even allowed to study the human body in the presence of men. She then starts focusing on mentally disabled children who, until then, were drawn from ordinary schools and considered "uneducable" due to their deficiencies.
>
> Against the general belief, Montessori is convinced that their problem is not so much medical, but rather pedagogical: when adequately stimulated, these children can improve greatly.

2. Transformative Vision: The Big "YES".

> Deeply inspired by her background in paediatrics as well as by her psychological, anthropological, and philosophical research, she calls for a complete transformation of educational methods. Montessori has a vision of Education strongly based on Science but aiming at the transformation and improvement of human beings.
>
> She strongly believes in Childhood Education as the master route to build a more compassionate Humankind and as a key to the reform of Society (Re-form is the capacity to give a new form, in other words to re-shape

a current situation). She defends "Education for Peace" or Education as a "Science of Peace", as she calls it.

The goal of the Montessori method is to develop the child's sensory and cognitive skills, while at the same time enhancing the child's practical life skills, natural abilities, own initiative and character – what we call connecting Heads, Hands and Heart.

In Montessori's view, each child has a unique potential for growth and development waiting to be expressed and revealed and such potential is best developed by letting the child be free to explore and manipulate the surrounding environment. She speaks about "deploying" a potential rather than moulding or formatting it.

As opposed to Education seen as formatting and conforming a child, her approach comes from the root of the word - Education in Latin is *Exducere*, "to lead outside". It is "unwrapping" and allow people to become "all they can be". Education becomes a process of "I Opening", "Eye Opening" and "High Hopening"!

The role of the teacher in this process should not be that of directing the child's activities, but rather that of continually adapting the environment in new and exciting ways in order to let the child fulfil his / her potentials — physically, cognitively, emotionally, and spiritually – at growing degrees of Complexity.

The Montessori method relies on a subtle interplay between Focus and Freedom, each of which would be meaningless without the other: Freedom according to the child's natural abilities and preferences. Focus, discipline and organization to channel the child's energy.

3. Anticipative Experimentation: Educate the Human Potential

In 1899, after beginning to disseminate her innovative ideas on child pedagogy at the national level, Montessori is asked to direct the State Orthophrenic School in Rome, where she continues her experiments and observations on how children reach new levels of autonomy and self-motivation to move up to new levels of Understanding.

Through the refinement of her methodology, she manages to lead some of her retarded children to pass State exams with the same performance as "normal" children.

This amplifies her questioning on the validity of the conventional system of Education for "normal" children. In 1906, she starts organizing a school for the children of indigent working mothers in the slums of Rome.

In 1907 the first "Casa dei Bambini" ("Children's House") is founded, and soon becomes a model school to be visited by educators and researchers from all over the world.

The "Montessori method" is born. Its accomplishments are popularized by the Press and quickly spread internationally.

It becomes the "Montessori Movement", followed worldwide by thousands of enthusiastic adopters. Schools, associations and societies are created all over the world: in Russia, in America, in Japan and India.

By the end of 1911, Montessori Education is officially adopted in public schools internationally.

As many Shapers, Maria Montessori generates strong resistance.

In 1936, Italy's fascist government condemns and proscribes the Montessori principles and closes all Montessori schools. Fleeing the Second World War, she moves to India where she will remain from 1936 to 1945. The qualities of her method, which transcends all cultural boundaries, explains the opening of numerous Montessori schools in India.

Between 1942 and 1944, she introduces the term "Cosmic Education" to describe an advanced course for children aged from six to twelve years that emphasizes the interdependence of all the elements of the natural world. This work leads to the publication of two books: "*Education for a New World*" and "*To Educate the Human Potential*".

She receives six nominations for the Nobel Peace Prize and multiple awards.

Although her influence has not been without resistance or hostility, the pioneering method of childhood Education she proposed – as early as 1908 – has survived almost unchanged in its essential features for more than ninety years and shown an amazing degree of resilience.

For instance, in the USA, its influence was seriously limited in the 1920's by two authoritative detractors. Forty years later, the Montessori approach knows a radical revival in a context where many parents are willing to play a much more active role in their children's Education.

In 2011, a wall street journal article wrote: [*Montessori...*]: *the surest route to joining the creative elite, which are so overrepresented by the schools' alumni that one might begin to suspect a Montessori mafia*"[72]

There must indeed be something specific in the "Montessori Thinking and method", to explain that, more than 100 years after its "debut", those who once were "Montessori children" seem so "fit for their time".

---

[72] The Montessori Mafia By Peter Sims, The Wall Street Journal, April 5, 2011

Montessori might be the only thing that the various people hereunder have in common

- Gabriel Garcia Marquez (Nobel Prizes in literature, he said "I do not believe there is a method better than Montessori for making children sensitive to the beauties of the world and awakening their curiosity regarding the secrets of life.")
- Erik Erikson (Danish-German American psychologist and psychoanalyst known for his theory on human social development, Erikson may be most famous for coining the phrase "identity crisis")
- Joshua Bell (Grammy award-winning violinist and of a Pulitzer prize-winning media story, he is famous for his experiences of playing the violin in the street to explore the true meaning of his work)
- Peter Drucker (Author, Management consultant, "social ecologist", awarded the presidential medal of Freedom, one of the most influential management gurus in History)
- Yo Yo Ma (A child prodigy cellist, United nations Peace Ambassador, winner of 15 Grammy Awards, Presidential Medal of Freedom & National Medal of the Arts)
- Roger Federer (Tennis champion, also well known for his calm and "elegance")
- Will Rights (Video game pioneer, says "SimCity comes right out of Montessori... It's all about learning on your own terms." [73])
- Whether you like their actions and realisations, it is also the case of Larry Page and Sergey Brin, the founders of Google, and of Jeff Bezos, Founder of Amazon.

---

[73] https://www.ted.com/talks/will_wright_spore_birth_of_a_game

Oh! We forgot... George Clooney (Academy award-winning actor, director, producer, humanitarian, United nations messenger of peace)

Montessori! What else?

Rosa Parks (United States 1913-2005) - Shaper of Social Justice and Freedom

We are in 1955, in the deeply segregated Montgomery, Alabama.

A seamstress by profession, Rosa Parks is imprisoned because, despite the "law" which obliges Afro-American citizens to sit at the back of the bus, she refuses to surrender the seat she occupies at the front of the bus to a white man.

In those days, almost a hundred years after Abraham Lincoln's Declaration of Emancipation (1863), which proclaimed the freedom of slaves, *"the Negro is still not free"*.

The deep South remains very segregated. As examples, Afro-American citizens are obliged to sit at the back of a bus, toilets and drinking fountains are separated, among many other examples.

The Ku Klux Klan is very active and all mighty. Acts of violence such as lynching, beating, bombing, burning of houses and churches immediately repress the slightest demonstration of rebellion.

Remember "Mississippi Burning", a 1988 film by Alan Parker with William Dafoe and Gene Hackman.

At one point, Birmingham, the capital of Alabama is renamed "Bombingham".

The majority of people conform with Segregation although it has been declared unconstitutional, first in the field of Education by the Supreme Court in May 1954.

Along with her husband, Rosa had long been active in the Civil Rights Movement. But the National Association for the Advancement of Coloured People - founded in 1909 to respond to all forms of violence against "coloured" people (today called Afro-Americans), was limited in its action in the

Deep South by the Ku Klux Klan which was more powerful than the Federal Government.

Other black people had already had the courage to challenge "Jim Crow".[74]

Jackie Robinson, the first black baseball player accepted in the professional league, back in 1944 (he made Life's magazine cover), who refused to be relinquished in the "coloured" section of a bus. Tried by a court martial, he was finally acquitted.

Nine months before Rosa Parks, a 15-year old schoolgirl by the name of Claudette Colvin had challenged Segregation on busses.

When asked why she is not better known, the reason Claudette evokes is that, at the time, she was a teenager and that the black representatives felt Rosa Parks would be a better and more "reliable" symbol of a population, while she would only have represented an "age bracket".

In 1955, Rosa Parks becomes the legendary woman who *"sat down so that we could stand up but not so we could stand still"* (Jesse Jackson).

The single action of this 42-year-old black seamstress in a Montgomery bus– which symbolizes a big "NO" of major importance - changes the course of a Nation, spurs a city-wide 385-day boycott and is the catalyst of the Long Civil Rights March, a nationwide effort to end segregation in public facilities and lead by Martin Luther King, then twenty-seven.

---

[74] "Jim Crow" was the expression used to designate a set of local and national laws assembled in the "Black Codes". Promulgated by the legislatures of the southern States from 1877 to 1964, the objective of these laws was to limit the efficiency of the constitutional rights black people had acquired after the War of Secession: the 13th Amendment to the Constitution (December 6th 1865) abolishing Slavery, the 14th Amendment of 1868 granting citizenship to any person born or naturalized in the United States and the 15th Amendment of 1870, guaranteeing the right to vote to all citizens of the United States.

THE ART OF SHAPERSHIP

All her life, Rosa remained a symbol of courage in the face of racial injustice.

Her story shows that you don't have to be a leader or someone important to do something important, to take a stand, to make an impact and change History.

In fact, she is an "Eye opener" and an "High Hopener". Her action generated a movement: a collective Big Yes and a series of Anticipative Experimentations.

She awakened the latent and unexpressed Big YES of the black population of Montgomery. Getting out of fatalisation, people suddenly regained confidence in themselves and dared.

This Big Yes was largely amplified by the launching of the Non-Violent Resistance Movement personified by Martin Luther King Junior who will, as everybody knows, bring it to its climax at the Civil Rights March on August 28th, 1963.

Never before had so many people, from so many geographical, social, cultural and racial origin assembled and marched towards a shared destination to manifest a common claim.

It is on this day that Martin Luther King Jr pronounced his "I have a Dream" historical speech, the title of which refers to the "Big Yes" many people in the public and in the country hoped for.

On that day, wherever she was looking from, Rosa Parks must have felt proud of the "unconscious" Shaper she had been eight years before!

Rosa left us on October 24th, 2005, fifty years after the Civil Rights Act (1964) and 150 years after the Declaration of Emancipation of Slaves by President Abraham Lincoln (1863).

On February 27th, 2013, President Obama inaugurated Rosa Park's statue in the Capitol's Statues Hall, emphasizing in his speech that he wouldn't have been elected President *"without the courage and obstination of the people who participated in Civil Rights movements back in the 50's and 60's".*

Rosa Parks is the first Afro-American woman to be honoured in such a way.

THE ART OF SHAPERSHIP

Martin Luther King (United States 1929 -1968) - Shaper of New Dreams

Born in Atlanta, Georgia on January 15th, 1929, Baptist Pastor Martin Luther King Jr. is assassinated on April 4th, 1968, in Memphis, Tennessee at age thirty-nine.

A rather short life span to contribute to the generation of deep changes in American Society and in the course of the United States' History!

1. Creative Resistance: The Big "NO".

Martin Luther King is an American clergyman, activist and one of the Leaders in the African American Civil Rights Movement. Like Rosa Parks and many others, he can no longer stand the shameful conditions of Poverty, Insecurity and Injustice under which the black populations live in the Southern States.

After the Rosa Park incident in 1955, Martin Luther King is chosen to symbolize Resistance. Probably inspired by Gandhi, he pioneers a "Creative Protest" based on Non-Violent Civil Disobedience.

2. Transformative Vision: The Big "YES".

Martin Luther King has a dream of a more peaceful and completely egalitarian world.

As he says:

> "Now is the time to rise from the dark and desolate valley of Segregation to the sunlit path of Social Justice".

A dream started in 1905 by the creation of a Movement (the NAACP, National Association for the Advancement of Colored People) which, at the time, answered the hopes and aspirations of millions of people.

Martin Luther King embodies a possible Future.

3. Anticipative Experimentation: Peaceful Resistance

Martin Luther King leads several marches followed by thousands of people, Blacks and Whites. Among which the "Long Civil Rights March", a nationwide effort to end segregation in public facilities.

The Transformative "Dream" he expresses in his memorable speech of August 28th, 1963 in front of the Lincoln Memorial in Washington DC, during the March for Employment and Freedom, clearly indicates the new Shape he has in mind.

At that time, he fully embodies a cause and a stance. It is probably on purpose that the Master of Ceremony introduces him as "the Moral Leader of the Nation".

He represents something powerful: a way forward, which means Progress, Social Justice and a new kind of Democracy. He makes people "march" with him for a better world. A world with more room to be and more room to grow for all. People follow him because he is holding their hopes. He is a "High Hopener"!

The Movement he and his friends launch, and support becomes so strong and so impressive that Dr. King becomes the youngest Nobel Peace Prize winner in 1964– at age thirty-five.

But his "Long March" doesn't have followers only. Though he chooses to fight racial inequality through non-violence, the changes he embodies and fights for generate such a strong resistance that a violent end is put to his life on April 4th, 1968.

His legacy is significant, multiform and irreversible.

His example inspired many individuals such as James Meredith (1933-) who was the first Afro-American student admitted in the segregated University of Mississippi and many others who became Shapers at their level, in their domain, and inspired others to become Shapers themselves

Most of all, he initiated a "Cultural Revolution": the transmission of a new Spirit both in his Community and in Society which, as a whole, was becoming more and more aware of the necessity of new shapes.

A very obvious aspect of Martin Luther King's legacy can be observed in the movie industry where actors like Sidney Poitier, another kind of Pioneer, was the first black actor to set his own standards: "To *make films about Dignity, Nobility and the Magnificence of Human Life*".

Having become one of the finest actors of his time, he also touched the conscience of millions of moviegoers across the Earth. Morgan Freeman, Forest Whitaker, Denzel Washington, and others proudly walked the trail he blazed and contributed to transform the image of a community referred to as "Uncle Toms" (1903) to men who proudly display the colour of their skin.

Nearly five decades later, this irreversible and increasing movement led to the election of the first Afro-American President of the United States: Barack Obama (1961-). If Dr. King and Rosa Parks hadn't been the kind of Shapers they were, President Obama would not have been there, experiencing other resistances to new shapes he would have liked to foster.

Pastor Jose Maria Arizmendiarrieta (1915 - 1976) - Shaper of a Regional destiny

Eldest son of a family of modest means, Arizmendiarrieta is deeply inspired by Faith and profoundly attached to his native Basque Country. He escapes military service due to the loss of an eye in a childhood accident. He becomes a journalist for "Eguna", a Basque language newspaper created in October 1936 which is the voice of the Basque Government.

A year later, after being informed against, he is thrown into jail.

Upon his release, he resumes his studies in Vitoria and returns to the Basque Country in February 1941 as a 26-year-old, newly ordained catholic priest (the previous one having been shot by Franco's forces).

1. Creative Resistance: The Big "NO".

He finds a town with a population of 7.000 people still suffering from the aftermath of the Spanish Civil War: severe unemployment, poverty, hunger, exile and tensions.

He finds this Reality unacceptable.

2. Transformative Vision: The Big "YES".

Determined to find a way to assist his congregation, he realizes that economic development - creating jobs - is the key to solve the town's other problems.

His Vision is deeply rooted in the social doctrine of the Catholic Church, in particular, the teachings regarding

- the Dignity of the human person and his or her labour
- Social Solidarity
- the primacy of Labour over Capital

3. Anticipative Experimentation: An Ecosystem of cooperatives and a Learning Region

Guided by these principles, he creates the Mondragon Cooperatives Movement (the Basque Country had a long tradition in coops). From the beginning of the Mondragon cooperatives, capital is used to benefit the workers-owners, exactly at the opposite of what happens in most for-profit Businesses where labour is hired at the service of capital.

In 1943, Jose Maria creates a technical college that becomes a training ground for generations of managers, engineers and skilled labour for local companies, and primarily for the cooperatives. He also spends a number of years educating young people about a form of Humanism based on Solidarity, Participation and the importance of acquiring the necessary technical Knowledge.

In 1955, he selects five of these young people to set up the first industrial company of the Mondragon Corporation.

At the end of 2012, Mondragon Corporation was still considered as "the corporation which resist crises", employed 83,321 people in 256 companies in four areas of activity: Finance, Industry, Retail and R&D.

Today, the Basque Country has become a "Learning and Innovation Region". Originally based on untraditional Governance mechanisms - a shared Mission, a philosophy of Cooperation (acting as owners and protagonists), Participation (commitment to Management), Solidarity (distribution of Wealth) and Innovation (constant renewal) - the whole Mondragon cooperation's culture and principles have long been a model.

Today, Jose Maria Arizmendiarrieta's heritage seems to have eroded: the organization has become an international holding like others and no longer defines itself as a solution to replace the capitalist system but as a "more humane and participative company".

The Creative Resistance and the Transformative Vision seem to have faded away.

THE ART OF SHAPERSHIP

Dr. Govindappa Venkataswamy (India 1918-2006) - Shaper of an Eye-Care System with a Vision

Dr. Govindappa Venkataswamy – known as Dr. V- made a career performing Eye-Care surgery at the Government Medical College in Madurai (South India).

At age fifty-five, plagued with advanced arthritis, he is forced to retire.

1. Creative Resistance: The Big "NO".

> Dr. V faces a horrific Reality: in India, twelve million people are blind and, as the Indian saying goes, "A blind person is a mouth with no hands." [75] Being blind in India is therefore a fatal disease. Under those conditions, a person is estimated to have two to three years to survive.
>
> Yet, 80 percent of this blindness is "useless". Understand: it could be avoided thanks to appropriate prevention and care.
>
> Dr. V decides to put an end to this unacceptable situation.

2. Transformative Vision: The Big "YES".

> Dr. V gives himself and his life a gigantic purpose, formulated in very simple terms:
>
> *"Eliminate Needless Blindness among India's Poors"*
>
> An aspiration which does not scare him, inspired largely by Gandhi's life and work, as well as by Sri Aurobindo's spiritual path.

---

[75] In 2018, "More than a billion people around the world need eyeglasses but don't have them, researchers say, an affliction long overlooked on lists of public health priorities. Some estimates put that figure closer to 2.5 billion people", New York Times, May 5th, 2018. https://www.nytimes.com/2018/05/05/health/glasses-developing-world-global-health.html

3. Anticipative Experimentation: An Ecosystem Strategy against Needless Blindness

In 1976, driven by his higher purpose, he founds the Aravind Eye-Care Hospital.

At that time, all he has are eleven beds, a shared aspiration which creates cohesion and a clear efficiency standard: surprisingly to all, he considers McDonald's as a source of inspiration on the efficiency side. If McDonald's can deliver the same hamburger all over the world, it must also be possible to train people and deliver high quality eye surgery to all those who need it all over the world.

The "elimination of Needless Blindness among India's Poors" requires providing high quality eye-care services at low prices. It requires an ecosystem approach in rural south India, deeply rooted in territorial realities and connected with local communities.

So, that's what Dr. V does.

Poor people are too poor to come to the hospital:

- He puts in place a network of hospitals, clinics, community outreach efforts to create an effective referral system in rural areas
    o women are trained for eye diagnosis
    o non-physicians gather diagnostic data and counsel patients
    o telemedicine centres, research and training institutes are created
- He organizes transportation services to and from the hospital for patients who must undergo surgery
- Upon arrival, each patient has the choice between paying or free accommodation structures. This has an impact on the sophistication of the accommodation but not on the quality of the medical treatments which

always remain the same. Most Aravind's patients (55 percent) only pay a symbolic participation or nothing at all. Each "paying" person covers the costs of two non-paying persons

- The process of cataract operation is streamlined, allowing it to be seven times faster than elsewhere and making it possible for doctors to conduct up to 100 operations a day with an unprecedented level of quality and efficiency worldwide (the operating ophthalmologist concentrates solely on the operation, everything else is taken care of by well-educated assistants)

- Once patients are there, they require custom-made glasses. Doctor V. creates a factory: building the necessary glasses on site is cheaper than importing them.

  Today, "*Aravind distributes each year 600.000 pairs of glasses in India and has extended its action to Nepal, Bangladesh and other countries through a network of local partners.*" Aravind has also created a manufacture of contact lenses, which allowed to reduce their price from 200 dollars per pair down to five dollars per pair for equal quality. Today, these lenses are sold in more than eighty-five countries, thus contributing to making quality ophthalmic products available in the world

- Dr. V. creates a network of hospitals and clinics along with R&D laboratories and training centres.

Started with eleven beds, Aravind Hospital has since grown into the world's largest provider of eye-care, "Aravind Eye-Care System", which is a model of efficiency, admired all over the world. It is not only a health success but also a financial success.

Today, the Aravind system manages some 2.5 million outpatient visits and 300,000 eye surgeries (It has been calculated that Aravind does 60 percent as many eye surgeries as the United Kingdom's National Health System per year, at one-hundredth of the cost). Aravind system makes enough on paid surgeries to not only cover the 55 percent of patients who cannot pay the market rates, but also to generate a nearly 40 percent gross operating margin.

Along all these years, the backbone of Aravind System has remained the same shared aspiration: "Eliminate Needless blindness among the Poors". What really drives efficiency at Aravind is the commitment to this higher purpose. [76] Such efficiency has allowed millions of the world's poorest citizens to have their sight restored.

In the meantime, Aravind decided to share their own practices with other hospitals to create their "own competition" as they say with a glimpse. What is the point of having such a purpose and to stay within "Business limits"? Convinced that their practice can help, they share them all over the world.

They generated a movement based on co-creation. So, they also expanded their purpose: The Vision 2020 is *"Eliminating preventable blindness worldwide"*.

They do all they can to make it happen.

---

[76] What can be learned from the developing world, Howard Larkin, Eurotimes, Volume 15, Issue 10. http://www.eurotimes.org/10October/managingeyecare.pdf

Muhammad Yunus (Bangladesh 1940-) - Shaper of the Nation through Credit for the Poor

Born on June 28th 1940 in Bangladesh, Nobel Prize winner Muhammad Yunus is brought up under British influence among his thirteen brothers and sisters. His father is a Gold broker.

He studies Economics in his country and obtains a Ph.D. in Economics at Vanderbilt University in the United States.

At age twenty-one, he has travelled practically all over the world.

At that time, he teaches in a college located in his area and he creates the first High-Technology factory. But Adventure calls and he returns to United States where he successfully acquires a master's degree, then a Doctorate followed by a thesis in Economy before obtaining a teaching position at Middle Tennessee State University.

His country having been involved in a war a year before, he decides to abandon his teaching position at Middle Tennessee and go back home, bringing his Knowledge and competences to help rebuild his country.

He first goes to work for the Bengladesh's New Government, then becomes head of Chittatong University Economics Department.

That is where he is going to launch a system which will build his worldwide reputation: the micro-credit. In 1977, the « Grameen » program is developed and launched. It is based on confidence in the less affluents by granting them access to Credit.

The Grameen organization becomes a Banking Institution in 1983 and, a few years later, the model begins to be exported outside the country.

1. Creative Resistance: The Big "NO".

Once home, he observes how unfair the Bangladeshi credit system is, excluding a large part of the population, too poor to qualify for traditional bank loans. For instance, women who make bamboo furniture have to take usurious loans to buy bamboo and repay their profits to the lenders. Traditional banks do not want to make tiny loans at reasonable interests to the poor due to high risk of default.

2. Transformative Vision: The Big "YES".

In 1976, during visits to the poorest households in a village, he discovers that very small loans could make a disproportionate difference to a poor person.

Yunus is persuaded that, given the chance, the poor will repay the money. An important part of his Vision emerges from his attitude: show trust in the Poor by giving them access to Credit.

His Big YES is born, foster economic and social development from the base up, thanks to Micro credit! He will dedicate his entire Life to make it succeed!

Yunus develops the concept of "Credit for the Poor", based on his new Business Model and on two completely new and unconventional loan mechanisms: Microcredit and Microfinance, co-developed with Dr. Akhtar Hameed Khan, founder of the Pakistan Academy for Rural Development (now Bangladesh Academy for Rural Development).

3. Anticipative Experimentation: Micro Credit for the Poor

In 1977, the « Grameen » Micro-credit program is launched. By the way, « Grameen » means Village.

The program serves two main purposes the second of which, often forgotten, is capital in making a difference:

- give access to an original loan system for people who are at the lowest end of the economic spectrum and, until then, are excluded from any system
- include the people in the redistribution of profits

In 1982, the institution is 28.000 members strong. And on October 1st, 1983, the pilot project begins operating as a full-fledged bank for poor Bangladeshis. It is renamed "Grameen Bank".

In 2006, this revolutionary approach to Banking wins Yunus and the Grameen Bank the Nobel Peace Prize *"for their efforts to create economic and social development from below through microcredit "*.

By July 2007, Grameen has issued $ 6.38 billion to 7.4 million borrowers.

In 2008, Yunus is rated #2 in Foreign Policy Magazine's list of the "Top 100 Global Thinkers".

Note that in 2018, the bank has over nine million borrowers. 97 percent of them are illiterate women.

In February 2011, together with Saskia Bruysten, Sophie Eisenmann and Hans Reitz, Yunus co-founds Yunus Social Business Global Initiatives (YSB), a project with an even broader and more ambitious objective, i.e. *"To create and empower Social Businesses to address and solve social problems around the world"*.

YSB is the international implementation arm for Yunus's Vision of a new, humane Capitalism. YSB starts managing Incubator Funds for social Businesses in developing countries and provides advisory services to companies, Governments, Foundations and NGOs.

Yunus's authority and "audience" make him a sort of "political" influence. This stimulates several reactions and a desire to reduce or even eliminate him from the "scene".

In March 2011, the Bangladesh Government fires Yunus from his position at Grameen Bank, citing legal violations and an age limit on his position. Bangladesh's High Court affirms his removal on March 8th. The allegations against Yunus become political when the Government of Bangladesh turns against him and the concept of Microfinance, accusing it of *"sucking blood from the poors"*.

It is interesting to read his declaration of 2018 about the origins of the enterprise

> *"It was to protect people from loan sharks in the villages," he says simply. He jokes about how they translated the Bangla word for it into "micro credit". "But maybe the terminology was wrong," he says, "Maybe I should have called it 'Nano credit', because the sums were so small."*[77]

Looking back, we can appreciate the originality and Creativity of Yunus's Economic Thinking. He built a bank that looked very different from its contemporaries (and still does), built on fundamentally different assumptions about Human beings and on a specific articulation of Creative Resistance, Transformative Vision and an original Business Model.

---

[77] https://www.hindustantimes.com/books/muhammad-yunus-at-jlf-2018-poverty-in-the-world-is-a-solvable-problem/story-bRWY3siZT8nrBCB-AQqrWqO.html

THE ART OF SHAPERSHIP

Customers are supposed to act in ways that help the Bank by forming groups and supporting each other to repay the loans and accumulate savings. They are supposed to value the Bank, not just as a source of cash but also as a Partner in navigating through Life.

This makes an enormous difference with some other denatured versions of Microcredit proposed by other financial institutions that are not inhabited by the same spirit, thus are not of the same nature…

In an article published in 2018 - "Poverty in the world is a solvable problem" -, the following quotes appear:

> "He does not like the idea of micro credit being used as a vehicle for profit, either. Venture capital without a need for profit is the "right" kind of micro credit".
> "But there is also a "wrong" micro-credit, he insists. Using micro-credit ventures to make profits off the poor", he insists" "is wrong".
> "The micro-credit Business is not for profit," he says aghast. "You'll end up becoming the loan shark we were trying to save people from."[78]

Muhammad Yunus is the author of several books including "Banker for the Poor" (1999), "Creating a world without poverty" (2007), the title of which indicates his capacity to have transformative Visions.

His last book published in 2017 is called "A World of Three Zeroes: the new economics of Zero Poverty, Zero Unemployment, and Zero Carbon emissions".

It is of course based on a "big NO" and on a Big "YES".

---

[78] https://www.hindustantimes.com/books/muhammad-yunus-at-jlf-2018-poverty-in-the-world-is-a-solvable-problem/story-bRWY3siZT8nrBCB-AQqrWqO.html

- The big "NO": the complete challenge of the current system of Capitalism
- The big "YES": a real trust in human beings and the belief that Poverty is a solvable problem.

As he says:

> *"All humans are creative entrepreneurs. The present concept of capitalism cannot accommodate the concept of social entrepreneurship because at the heart of the capitalist philosophy is the idea that human beings are inherently selfish and will only work for their own greed. This system needs to be fixed. If everyone were an entrepreneur, then no one could exploit each other."*

A 80-year-old Shaper who has kept his Faith and his convictions.

Sanjit "Bunker" Roy (India, 1945-) - Shaper of Barefoot Education

Sanjit 'Bunker' Roy receives his formal Education in the Doon School (1956-62) and St. Stephens College Delhi University (1962-1967). He is Indian's National Squash Champion in 1965, 1967 and 1971.

As he says, *"I had a very elitist, snobbish, expensive Education in India, and that almost destroyed me."*

1. Creative Resistance: The Big "NO"

Sanjit "Bunker" Roy is in his twenties during the 1960's, when famine hits the Indian villages of the region of Bihar. He acts then as a volunteer.

"Several thousands of people died of hunger. That experience changed my life."

His "real" Education starts when he digs open wells for drinking water as an unskilled labourer for five years (1967-1971). It is there that he becomes conscious of what he calls

"The power of the Knowledge of the least privileged, the most extraordinary knowledge there is".

One day, Sanjit "Bunker" Roy realizes that Development projects all over the world run into one crucial point: for a project to live on, it needs to be organic, owned and sustained by those it serves. "Bunker" is confronted with the separation between the Elite and the poor populations in India. This leads him to think about how to overthrow the status quo and redefine the way the world thinks about fighting Poverty.

2. Transformative Vision: The Big "YES"

Sanjit "Bunker" Roy is a great believer in Mark Twain who said, *"Never let School interfere with your Education"*.

No need to attend the great schools to achieve great things. Bunker wants to put Trust in that Wisdom and that Knowledge of the Poor.

> *"When you think about it, what is a professional? Someone who embodies a blend of knowledge, of self-confidence and of faith. It is even the least privileged who possess that professionalism "because they cannot read nor write, many are under the impression they don't possess the knowledge or Wisdom necessary to their own development.".*[79]

Inspired by the life and work of Gandhi, Sanjit's goal is to make rural communities in India self-sufficient by learning how to generate heat, to create light, to access drinking water, to heal and to get out of Poverty.

3. Anticipative Experimentation: The Barefoot College

In 1972, in the village of Tilonia in Rajasthan, "Bunker" creates "Barefoot College", the only College in India where rural women and men – many of them illiterate – are taught to become solar engineers, architects, artisans and doctors.

There are only two rules for enrolment: to attend, you must be poor, and you must take your learnings home to your village.

---

[79] Cited in an interview given in October 2017 « quality of life » conference, London.

> "We believe in the traditional way of solving problems. If there is a shortage of drinking water, instead of installing an arm pump, we collect rainwater."

As he describes it,

> "Barefoot College is a place of Learning and Unlearning, where the Teacher is the Learner and the Learner is the Teacher."

Barefoot College is the only University in India where Traditional Knowledge and practical skills of the poor are given more importance and priority than paper degrees or qualifications. This is an illustration of a leap in confidence made to the people and by the people to themselves.

At Barefoot College, the "Barefoot Solutions" can be broadly categorized into

- Solar Energy
- Access to Water
- Education
- Health care for local treatment
- Rural Handicrafts
- People's action
- Communication
- Women's Empowerment
- Wasteland Development.

The University has stood up for the past thirty years. *"The first stone was laid in 1989. The building costs were limited to 22.000 dollars. It is the only University in the world to operate exclusively on solar energy. Five solar panels generate enough energy to operate thirty computers, 500 bulbs, 100 ventilators, a refrigerator, a fax, telephones and two routers".*[80]

---

[80] http://www.wired.co.uk/article/disrupting-poverty, Wired Magazine, 7th March 2011

Started in India, the demystified and decentralized community-based Barefoot approach has been implemented in over thirty of the Least Developed Countries. A total of 50,000 houses in more than 1.200 villages have been solar electrified by nearly 300 illiterate rural grandmothers who, using only sign language, have successfully been trained in six months to be solar engineers able to bring Electricity to their remote villages.

Sanjit "Bunker" Roy has been identified as one of the fifty environmentalists who could save the Planet by The Guardian in 2008 and as one of the 100 most influential people in the world by Time magazine in 2010 for having trained over three million people as Solar Engineers, Teachers, midwives and in weaving, architecture, and medicine.

Another great example of Shapership™!

Chris Rufer (United States, 1949-) - Shaper of Self-Management

You probably never heard of Chris Rufer, but you most probably tasted or used one of the products he is associated with: like Ketchup, tomato paste, diced tomatoes, just to name some examples.

A Student in Economics at UCLA in California, Chris Rufer begins his professional career as a one-man owner/operator trucking company, hauling tomatoes from field to factory during his summer breaks.

Years later, Morning Star, his company has become one of the largest processors of tomatoes in the United-States. Above all, it is an exceptional company, based on a libertarian Philosophy and self-Management practices totally new at the time.

1. Creative Resistance: The Big "NO".

> At that time, many organizations are – and still are today – managed according to the Dinosaur's principles of Command-and-Control inherited from the industrial Revolution.
>
> While studying Economics at the University of California, he discovers and adopts principles that challenge "Conventional Wisdom" about Business: the most durable and efficient human enterprises are those which are built on Self-Management and Total Responsibility!
>
> They absolutely refuse hierarchical, pyramidal structures and their traditional corollaries such as Supervision, and Control.

2. Transformative Vision: The Big "YES"

Very early in his career, Chris develops a Vision and a Business Philosophy around a fundamental cornerstone which simply states that Self-Management is the most effective and efficient method of organizing people.

He imagines a company built on that principle, where professionals can self-organize, take initiatives and coordinate their activities between themselves, with their suppliers, their clients, without any supervision nor directions. Why should such an organization be more efficient? Because it becomes a place where Joy, Pride and the Excitement of creating together, of putting everyone's talents to work to reinforce and complete the talents of others are present and encouraged! As well as taking initiatives and full responsibility for them!

As Chris Ruffer puts it:

> *"Self-Management starts and ends with the premise that in order to achieve greater productivity and engagement, people should not employ force against others and should keep their commitments. Self-Management principles simply respect the way we already live our lives outside of work. In our personal lives, we make all kinds of crucial, life-changing decisions without a boss: where to go to college, who to marry, what to do for a living.*
>
> *If employees know what to do and how to do it, why do they need managers?"*[81]
>
> *"Self-Management is developing structure from what most people call "below" versus dictated from above. It's a spontaneous*

---

[81] Beyond Empowerment: The Age of the Self-Managed Organization, Dough Kirkpatrick

development; it's about how you develop structure, not whether you have structure".

3. Anticipative Experimentation: A self-managed company

Chris develops his trucking operation, and in 1982, develops a partnership with a group of tomato growers to build a revolutionary tomato factory based on self-management.

This is Morning Star, a revolutionary plan, based on his Vision!

In fact, it becomes evident that, contrary to what a majority of people may imagine, Self-Management principles are going to help this plant reach a level of Efficiency never obtained until then in the Industry!

In 2010, Morning Star becomes *world leader in tomato production and processing, a company*

> *"whose revenues reached over $700 million in 2010 and where no one has a boss, where employees negotiate responsibilities with their peers, everyone can spend the company's money, and each individual is responsible for procuring the tools needed to do his or her work, where there are no titles and no promotions, compensation decisions are peer-based."* [82]

At morning Star, Self-Management applies both to highly educated scientists working with plant biology and to the colleagues harvesting tomatoes in the field. Morning

---

[82] Gary Hamel, "First, let's fire all the managers", Harvard Business Review, December 2011

Star proves that it is not only Knowledge workers who can be trusted to manage their work.

They are the world's leading producer of tomatoes, and continue to thrive, with every colleague leading his or her part of the mission.

Like a Jazz combo, Morning Star is an agile organization based on a remarkable good balance between Focus and Freedom:

- Focus: what holds the Company together are its Strategy and Culture. Its essential foundation and Cohesion factors are its shared Principles, Self-Management, its purpose, its processes and a Culture of Learning and Coaching
- Add to that the essential leap in Faith: Trust, supported by appropriate commitment and dialogue mechanisms, such as the Colleague Letter of Understanding (CLU)
- and you can see Freedom and "Self-Management" emerge: Distributed Leadership, Entrepreneurship and Creativity. Without any visible structure, and no unilateral authority to fire anyone

What this story illustrates is well-known but too rarely put into place:

It is not a question of practicing Empowerment, which in itself is a sort of patronizing attitude, inferring that some people have the power to transfer Power to others. Here it is the question of creating the conditions under which people can exert their Power!

As Dough Kirkpatrick says,

> *"Going beyond empowerment means that people have all the power they need to*

> *perform effectively from the very moment they join an organization, regardless of the level of responsibility or complexity.*
>
> *They are immune from threats or coercion. They are free to seek any needed resources or relationships on their own initiative. They are free to develop themselves and advance organizational learning. Ultimately, they are responsible for results to themselves, their peers and the organization's mission."* [83]

As soon as people understand where the organization is headed and why, as well as how they can contribute to that Strategy, as soon as they trust and are trusted, leaders can move away from Command and Control power mechanisms and see individuals lead themselves with Integrity and Authenticity.

Leaders then truly open new ways to be humane. They become Shapers.

And as we said earlier, Shapers don't empower. They "share" power.

Chris's drive for maximized efficiencies and his willingness to challenge all assumptions and norms lead the group to build a factory that truly revolutionized the Industry.

The Self-Management principles around which Chris shaped his company have proven to be a long-term competitive advantage.

Chris created the Self-Management Institute in 2008 as a Research and Education organization, the Mission of which "is to develop superior principles and systems of organizing people, and to instil those principles and systems in the minds of our client colleagues. "

---

[83] Beyond Empowerment: The Age of the Self-Managed Organization, Dough Kirkpatrick

He serves as a director of the Institute, plays an active role in the development of systems and educational programs and in applied Behavioral Research.[84]

---

[84] http://self-managementinstitute.org/index.php/about-us/chris-j-rufer/

Baltasar Garzón (Spain, 1955-) - Shaper of Universal Justice

1. Creative Resistance: The Big "NO"

Born in 1955, Baltasar Garzón is brought up in an Andalusian family of peasants with limited resources but attached to strong values of Solidarity. As a young boy, he hears stories told by the elders about the Civil War and the innumerable injustices of Franco's Dictatorship.

This drives him to make two major decisions:

- do everything he can to prevent these injustices from happening again
- and to categorically refuse to find any justification to violence.

2. Transformative Vision: The Big "YES"

Garzón studies Law and decides to become a Judge. In 1988, aged thirty-three, he is appointed investigating magistrate at the Central Court of Criminal Proceedings Number five, the highest penal jurisdiction in Spain.

He belongs to the generation which decides to commit sometimes at the cost of their lives against the violent repression of Franco's Regime.

As Garzón says:

> *"It was our way to change the World, to act in order to help Spanish Society to move from its submissive and obedient attitude generated by the fear of Power, to a new state of Consciousness oriented towards a new Destiny."*

3. Anticipative Experimentation: By the Law for the Law

Garzón becomes one of the most renowned magistrates in the world, so much driven by a deep faith in Democracy and Justice that national boundaries and foreign jurisdictions fail to stop him.

He fights "by the Law for the Law". And with exceptional courage, he dares to attack all forms of violations of Human Rights, of taboos, of traffics (arms and drugs), money laundering, terrorism, and corruption.

As the world's foremost practitioner of Universal Jurisdiction, he manages to make a breach in the fight against impunity of war crimes and of crimes against Humanity.

Until then, Heads of State and high-ranking military officers benefited from a broad immunity. Not only during but also after their mandates, in conformity with the "Act of State" doctrine.

In 1997, Garzón initiates pursuits for genocide against employees of the Argentinian Junta, responsible for the death or the disappearance of some 30.000 people during the period 1976 to 1983. He launches an international arrest notice against Leopoldo Fortunato Galtieri, one of the Argentinian Military Junta members.

On October 16th, 1998, he launches another international arrest notice against Chile's ex-dictator Augusto Pinochet for assassinations and tortures against Chilean citizens as well as for launching the sadly famous "Condor" operation during which a significant number of democrats and left-wing militants disappeared between 1973 and 1990 in Chile, Argentina, Uruguay and Brazil.

This is his way to pay Justice to thousands of victims and to History, so that no "negationist" candidate anywhere can pretend and say: *"This never happened!"*.

Garzón becomes a "Magistrate without Boarders", known worldwide as the pioneer of Defense of International Law and of Human Rights.

His Big "NO" and his Big "YES" take multiple shapes through his courageous actions, which all affirm the primacy of Law over Politics.

Among others:

- In 2001, he cites Silvio Berlusconi in front of the Council of Europe for Tax evasion

- In 2002, he launches an international Letter Rogatory in order to hear Henry Kissinger, ex-US Secretary of State, on his connections with the "Condor" operation in South America

- In 2003, he takes position against the war in Iraq, which he considers to be a violation of International Law and accuses the people responsible for this "Aggression War", among them George W. Bush, Tony Blair and José Maria Aznar, then Prime Minister of Spain

- From his position in Spain, he goes after some of the most important criminal cases in his own country, including terrorism, organized crime, arms trafficking, money laundering and even, in the 1980s, his own government's dirty war against militant Basque separatists whom he also charges for Terrorism

- In 2008, following the request of families and organizations of Victims, he proposes to apply the principles he has developed for the rest of the world to Spain. He launches an investigation into the disappearance of an estimated 114,000 people during Spain's 1936-39 civil war and the early years of Franco's dictatorship. In doing so, he attacks one of Spain's major taboos: the "Historic Memory" of that era. Three extreme right-wing organizations file complaint against Garzón, under the pretext that his investigation violates the 1977 Amnesty Law for crimes committed under the Franquist Dictatorship. He is threatened of being suspended

- In April 2009, he opens an enquiry against six members of the previous Government of the United States, responsible for acts of Torture and who endeavoured to reformulate these acts to juridically legitimate them. One of his last cases involved officials within the Popular Party, back to power since 2009, involved in a massive corruption scandal

Through his courage and his actions, Baltasar Garzón has become the symbol of a Universal Justice and a nightmare for the "Injusts". He has contributed to the development of a planetary Conscience concerned by the absolute necessity of International Law and the respect of Human Rights.

Of course, after having disturbed many circles through his "sensitive" investigations, he did not only make friends!

In his book *"A world without Fear"* (2005), he describes the professional consequences he was submitted to due to his positions. He tells about his life harassed by lobbies, defamed by unscrupulous lawyers, full of traps laid by politicians and media. He knew there would be a price to pay yet he never hesitated to serve his duties as a citizen and as a man of Law and Justice.

In his other book *"La Fuerza de la Razón"* (2011), Garzón evokes the notion of "Víctima Universal" (Universal Victim). To him, anyone becomes a victim when a crime is committed somewhere.

His second chapter starts with a sentence of Montesquieu:

> *"An injustice against anyone is a menace for all of us".*

Since 2010, the special treatment he gets in his own country looks like a witch-hunt. In May 2010, he is suspended from his functions. In February 2012, he is barred from practicing Law for eleven years, found guilty of having ordered the police to record conversations between inmates and their lawyers (The suspects were indicted for high-level corruption in a scandal that had tarnished the right-wing party, back in power in 2009. Garzón suspected the lawyers of laundering their clients' money).

This decision, taken unanimously by the seven members of the Supreme Court, means the career of a fifty-six-year-old man who dedicated his life to Justice was stopped by his peers. *"Which means that of all those involved in the massive corruption scandal, only the judge who pursued its investigation has been condemned."*[85] Hundreds of supporters gathered in the centre of Madrid to protest against this decision.

Requested by his own peers, the fall of Baltasar Garzón creates a threat to Justice - not only as a profession but also as a Value and an Ideal - and a menace to Democracy. Another illustration of how much a dominant system fights to maintain its own shape.

But Garzón is not the "abandoning" type! Suspended from Magistracy, he becomes a lawyer.

---

[85] Sentencing Spain's 'Super judge': Why Baltasar Garzón Is Being Punished, By Lisa Abend / Madrid Friday, Feb. 10, 2012 Time World. http://www.time.com/time/world/article/0,8599,2106537,00.html

In 2012, the previous Spanish judge engages in a new fight," *illustrating a desire for Change so intense that it neglects his own interests and own comfort."* [86]

He becomes the lawyer of Julian Assange, the founder of Wikileaks, an organization which, since 2006, publishes confidential documents in a civic information perspective, well-known and praised by the advocates of free access to information and transparency of public action and loathed by large corporations and governments who prefer to "dance in the dark". (In April 2017 for example, Mike Pompeo, head of the CIA, called Wikileaks a *"hostile Intelligence Service".*)

In 2010, following the publication of several tens of thousands of military documents which shed a blunt light on the behaviours of the American army in Afghanistan, Julian Assange is accused by the United States of being a spy and threatened of being extradited by the CIA. He is jointly charged by Sweden of sexual assault.

In 2012, Assange finds refuge at the Embassy of Ecuador in London to escape arrest and a possible extradition to the United States where preliminary instruction of his case is underway.

Garzón is the ideal lawyer! Capable of solving a complex international case in which Justice and high political spheres interact. With a unique access to the Ecuadorian Embassy, both men combined their forces for several years now, in their war in favour of the freedom of Internet, the protection of personal data and the freedom of Speech.

---

[86] Le Soir, 26/03/2018, Julian Assange et Baltasar Garzón contre le monde, http://plus.lesoir.be/147783/article/2018-03-26/julian-assange-et-baltasar-Garzón-contre-le-monde

THE ART OF SHAPERSHIP

This fight is significant because of its deep political implications and the conclusion of which will affect the freedom of Press all over the world. [87]

By the way, Garzón's office was burglarized on December 2017!!!

In 2015, Garzón denounces the systematic corruption in a book published in Spanish and the title of which can be translated as *"Filth: 40 years of corruption is Spain"*. He writes

> *"In all facets of public and private life in Spain, some '"affairs" have demonstrated that the phenomenon of corruption has deeply penetrated and impregnated each of our institutions and that answers to questions have been less than satisfactory".*

In August 2017, he creates the citizen's political platform "ACTUA", literally "Act". The objective is to generate the fall of the Spanish Right Wing in power thanks to a large coalition of the Left forces.

Garzón, a man for whom there is not the thickness of a cigarette paper of difference between his vision and his actions, leads his life with a rectitude and a courage which are be inspirational.

He has been honoured with twenty-two Doctorates Honoris Causa between 1999 and 2009.

---

[87] By the way, as most people know, after a 7-year period spent inside the Ecuador embassy in London, Julian Assange was arrested on April 11th, 2019, after the Ecuadorian President decided to withdraw his asylum status. He was taken to jail and in May, was sentenced to 50 weeks in jail for breaching his bail conditions. Later that year, he was faced with the reopening of the 2010 rape allegation by Swedish prosecutors.

Today, he is still fighting against his extradition to the US which will certainly lead to a long sentence in jail, whoever is elected as President.

Of course, 21 of them came from non-Spanish academic institutions (16 from Spanish-speaking countries, 2 from the USA and one from Belgium).

On November 9th, 2009, and for the first time in his life, he received an Honoris Causa in his own country.

Above all, Garzón leads an "unquiet" life so that we can live ours in a quieter way!

He fights so we can be freer!

THE ART OF SHAPERSHIP

Catia Bastioli (Italy, 1957-) - Shaper of a new model of Sustainable Development integrated with the Territory

Born in Foligno in 1957, Catia Bastioli graduates in Pure Chemistry in 1981 from the University of Perugia where she obtains top marks. In 1985, she starts attending the School of Business Administration at the Milan Boccioni University.

Since then, Catia Bastioli has won numerous international awards for her discoveries in the field of starch-based biodegradable materials; most notably, on April 18, 2007 she was nominated for the "European Inventor of the Year Prize" for her patents filed in the years 1992-2001, including Mater-Bi, the Bioplastics commercialized by Novamont.

Today, she is Chairman and Chief Executive Officer of Novamont, an Italian company founded in 1989 as a Research Centre, incubating Innovation, Research and Development in the field of Bioplastics.

1. Creative Resistance: The Big "NO".

Due to EU decisions, more than 800.000 hectares [88] of agricultural land are left uncultivated in Italy. Farmers get compensation from the European Union not to exploit their land whereas, in theory, these hectares of land could be converted into maize and oleaginous plants cultures and produce approximately two million tons of Bioplastics.

Catia Bastioli is convinced that the main challenge facing the new millennium is to find innovative development models, which are capable of preserving the planet's resources, whilst maintaining and improving the quality of life for its inhabitants.

---

[88] Close to 2 million acres

Confronted with the under exploitation of human and natural resources, she declares:

> *"Land is a limited resource. It is key that lead sectors with high potential and which can better leverage the local Biodiversity be considered as a key priority within the broader debate of Bioeconomy in Europe and in Italy.*
>
> *We need to encourage the creation of a Bioeconomy not based on subsidies but based on cutting-edge applications which respect stringent standards, and which can contribute to lower pressure on the Planet limited resources".*

2. Transformative Vision: The Big "YES".

Catia Bastioli thinks big, local and different!

Her Vision relies on a shift in perspective, a new way to think about Economy, the Territory and Environmental Sustainability:

> *"If we want to enable a real Revolution when tackling industrial policy, it is our mindsets and approaches that need to change. We need a Cultural Revolution and we need to work together in synergy in order to enable our Economies to work sustainably and enabling people to live better with less."*

What she commits to is

> *"Development integrated with the Territory".*

She wants the creation of a sustainable and inclusive model, involving the whole of Society, able to shape a new system of thinking about development from an environmental AND social perspective, creating new high-quality jobs, Growth and Prosperity in rural areas.

She envisions the transition from a Product-based Economy to a System-based Economy, built on the wise use of natural resources, technologies and Innovation.

> "Today, even more so than in the Past, we need a systematic view and a strategy which places Mankind and his Environment at the center rather than profit via the adoption of exceedingly high-quality standards and a system-based rather than a product-based rationale. The new approach must be informed by local circumstances and must involve all players. Intelligent researchers and entrepreneurs are also essential in the renewable raw materials sector, but without the active involvement of the entire local region and without rigorous system standards which are actively complied with, we run a very real risk of the sector being abused."

Thanks to her background, she senses the potential Nature provides in abundance: an enormous range of renewable raw materials - such as vegetable oils, starch from corn and potatoes, cellulose from straw and wood, lignin and amino acids – which can be converted into fuel, chemical intermediates, polymers and specialties in general, for which mineral oil has been used to date.

She sees how, by resorting to physical, chemical and biological processes, the development of products from renewable raw materials may represent a significant contribution to Sustainable Development in light of the potential for using less energy to produce them and in light of the wider range of waste disposal options with low environmental impact.

She also sees how all these elements represent a golden opportunity for developing vertically integrated systems, hopefully involving both farmers and industrial Businesses in a joint development effort with low environmental input and high societal benefits.

3. Anticipative Experimentation: Beyond core Business, infinite resources for the development integrated to the territory

She starts by focusing on local biodiversity and ecosystems – Natural and Human - with a Life Cycle Thinking approach. The aim is to act in synergy with them, multiplying opportunities provided by enhancing the value of local areas and creating strong co-operation and interactions with all the local players involved in the Value chain.

Implemented with determination, the Novamont concept of local bio-refineries integrated into the local area is emblematic: investigating a range of vegetable materials and local waste products and by-products, with an integrated supply chain rationale, reducing the need for transport as much as possible and maximizing the creation of knowledge circuits and integrated products with the various local players, such as farmers, local authorities, Universities, R&D centres, high schools, voluntary associations, the agricultural sector, small and medium scale companies and Society.

As an example, Novamont creates a collaboration and a joint company with Coldiretti, a cooperative composed of 600 local farmers, in order to maximize the specialization of cultivations, using all the relative discards and shortening the Value chain.

Having noticed that acres of non-cultivated surfaces are invaded by thistle, she initiates a totally innovative Creative Experimentation, in coherence with her Vision.

Thistle is generally considered as a weed and destroyed with drastic herbicides or fire.

Contrary to this habit, Catia Bastioli launches an in-depth study on the plant.

Rather than destroying Thistle, what else could be done with it? Well! Create multiple cash flows, for example:

- A lubricant for precision mechanics present in the flower
- A plastic made with the fiber contained in the stem
- A natural herbicide which, for information, has been chosen in 2018 to replace Monsanto's Round up in France.
- An enzyme covering the leaves to produce Pecorino cheese
- Feed for stock at 250 €/Ton versus 600 €/Ton for Chinese soy
- An elastomer in the roots to be included in tire manufacturing

Thanks to the curiosity and creativity of Catia Bastioli who dares think outside the prisons and the dogmas of the "core" Business, the various elements of the plant that were traditionally destroyed now generate a variety of revenue flows amounting to a total of 4200 Euros per ton! It also gives jobs to hundreds of people.

Today, Novamont is engaged in two important reconversion projects in Italy.

The logic behind them is to act in areas which are being badly hit by the current forms of crisis, where factories are inactive and human resources with high skills and know-how are often not valorised. The aim is to convert those plants in Biorefineries where Innovation and investments can unleash local Growth.

For example, in Adria (Veneto), Novamont is converting a plant into a first-of-a-kind flagship Biorefinery which will be dedicated to the production of bio BDO in partnership with Genomatica.

In Porto Torres (Sardinia), in association with Eni Versalis, Novamont is currently working and investing 500 million Euros on the conversion of a large petrochemical site into a third generation Biorefinery with an integrated and local supply chain in close collaboration with farmers, research centres and Universities.

Novamont Biorefinery is a new experimental model which creates an integrated system among industry, agriculture, environment and local economy, turning an entire region into an experimentation and Learning area.

This model can be reproduced in other territories, according to the availability of the appropriate cultures and attention brought to the environmental quality of the territory itself.

As Catia Bastioli says,

> *"Novamont is a genuine laboratory in every sense of the word in which I was lucky enough to develop my skills, to see people around me develop their skills and which allowed me to create a unique experience to assist those who wish to take part in this system-based economic experiment. Today, the challenge for Novamont is to become a catalyst for this country's development in this sector, fully implementing the "Bio-refinery model*

closely linked to the Territory" by working in partnership with the agricultural, industrial, institutional and academic sectors.

We hope that our experience can also be of benefit in defining our country's development strategy in the renewable raw materials sector, with an approach which demonstrates a level of **Wisdom** *which has to go much deeper than in the past."*Ricardo Semler (Brazil, 1959-) - Shaper of Industrial Democracy

Ricardo Semler is a Brazilian entrepreneur, CEO of SEMCO.

He is the son of Antonio Semler, a Brazilian engineer entrepreneur of Austrian origin and creator of SEMCO, a company originally specialized in supplying the Brazilian Navy.

Although his original plans were to become a Rock & Roll bassist, Ricardo Semler studies Law at São Paulo's University, the city where he was born.

After graduation and at the request of his father, he goes to work for the company which is going through great difficulties. He rapidly clashes with him for several reasons. One being that his father exerts a traditional autocratic style of Management.

Tired of these clashes, Ricardo threatens to leave the company. Rather than seeing this happen, his father resigns as CEO and vests majority ownership in his 21-year-old son in 1980.

Under Ricardo's guidance and after a difficult start, Semco undergoes a deep transformation and starts making remarkable progress: from 4 million dollars turnover in 1982 to over 200 million in 2003.

Ricardo Semler explains this success by his peculiar Management system: Industrial Democracy.

A system based on "Radical Wisdom" which grants more Freedom and more initiatives to the overall workforce members.

This enables the reduction of the intermediary Management structure and increases the responsibilization of the work force for everyone's and the company's benefits.

1. Creative Resistance: The Big "NO"

At SEMCO, Ricardo is shocked by what he calls the "Prison atmosphere":

> *"Thousands of rules work fine for an army or a prison system, but not for a Business. And certainly not for a Business that wants people to think, innovate and act as human beings"*[89].

Ricardo also disagrees with his father and his Board's belief that only highly specialized companies will survive and win. Ricardo advocates diversification away from the struggling shipbuilding Industry.

So, at age twenty-one, young Ricardo takes over a company that is on the verge of bankruptcy, threatened by reductions of volumes in the naval Industry and by Semco's high specialization, plagued by inefficiencies, baronies, low productivity, and low employee morale.

On his first day as CEO, he fires 60 percent of all top managers! On the commercial level, he decides that the "Specialization" paradigm is "out' and immediately begins working on a diversification program to rescue the company. In that short period of time, Semco purchases five new companies and extends its product line.

During his first four years as CEO, Ricardo is busy 24/7 running the company. Camping out in his office at times, he embodies his motto, "You either work hard, or you're out."

Yet, despite all these efforts, the company is not prospering, weakened by all its old disabling culture, habits and operating modes.

---

[89] Marquardt, Michael and Nancy Berger, Global Leaders for the 21st Century, (Albany: State University of New York Press 2000), 51

When he reaches twenty-five, a sudden fainting spell scares him and leads him to make a choice: either continue on his stress voyage or change his life. Ricardo decides to change.

This inspires him to opt for a greater balance between professional and personal life, not only for himself but everyone in the company.

He thinks that no one on his deathbed will ever say, "I wish I had spent more time at the office". He puts his life on a quest for Radical Wisdom and a leap of Faith over loss of control to invent a new kind of organization

2. The Transformative Vision: The Big "YES"

From then on, Ricardo imagines how to introduce Industrial Democracy in the workplace, treating all employees as responsible adults who can be trusted.

> *"In a word, we hire adults, and then we treat them like adults. Think about that. Outside the factory, workers are men and women who elect governments, serve in the army, lead community projects, raise and educate families, and make decisions everyday about the future.*
> *Friends solicit their advice. Salespeople court them. Children and grandchildren look up to them for their wisdom and experience.*
> *But the moment they walk into the factory, the company transforms them into adolescents. They have to wear badges and name tags, arrive at a certain time, stand in line to punch the clock or eat their lunch, get permission to go to the bathroom, give lengthy explanations every time they're five minutes late, and*

> *follow instructions without asking a lot of questions" (...)*
> *I believe in responsibility but not in pyramidal hierarchy.*
> *I think that Strategic Planning and Vision are often barriers to success.*
> *I dispute the value of Growth. I don't think a company's success can be measured in numbers, since the numbers ignore what the end-user really thinks of the product and what the people who produce it really think of the company. I question the supremacy of Talent, too much of which is as bad as too little. I'm not sure I believe that Control is either expedient or desirable."* [90]

3. Anticipative Experimentation: Radical Wisdom at work

His deep commitment to profound, respectful and democratic Change leads him to install practices unheard of before and for which he is known around the world today.

To operate the transition from a rigid and autocratic to a more democratic system, one of Ricardo's first undertakings is to dismantle the old pyramidal structure.

The twelve layers of Management are replaced by three concentric circles.

Gradually, as minds open and confidence settles in, old rules are replaced by "Extreme Common Sense"....

> *"I did try to reconstruct the company so that Semco could govern itself on the basis of*

---
[90] Harvard Business Review, Managing Without Managers, (1989)

three Values: Employee Participation, Profit-Sharing, and Open Information Systems." "*Participation gives people control of their work, Profit-Sharing gives them a reason to do it better, Information tells them what's working and what isn't*".

To give a few examples:

- Workers set their own production quotas
- They decide among themselves the best time to come to work
- They redesign the products they make, their work environments, and even formulate their own marketing plans
- Managers run their units with unheard of Freedom and determine Business Strategies without interference from top Management
- Each division in the company is allowed to set their own salary structure
- All financial information is discussed openly and freely
- If employees need assistance in making sense of the financial aspects, classes are held to assist them in understanding the meaning of the numbers
- There are reception desks but no receptionists
- There are no secretaries or personal assistants
- There are no executive dining rooms and no personalized parking spaces.
- For those whose job requires travel, there are no travel restrictions other than using your head
- There are no departments, no rules, and no audits. The entire budget system has been simplified

THE ART OF SHAPERSHIP

- Semco managers and workers make decisions together; anyone can participate to board meetings.

Here is another example of radical Wisdom in Practice:

> *On Mondays and Thursdays, I learn how to die. I call them my terminal days. My wife Fernanda doesn't like the term, but a lot of people in my family died of melanoma cancer and my parents and grandparents had it. And I kept thinking, one day I could be sitting in front of a doctor who looks at my exams and says, "Ricardo, things don't look very good. You have six months or a year to live."*
> *And you start thinking about what you would do with this time. And you say, "I'm going to spend more time with the kids. I'm going to visit these places; I'm going to go up and down mountains and places and I›m going to do all the things I didn't do when I had the time.» But of course, we all know these are very bittersweet memories we're going to have. It's very difficult to do. You spend a good part of the time crying, probably. So, I said, I'm going to do something else.*
>
> *Every Monday and Thursday, I'm going use my terminal days. And I will do, during those days, whatever it is I was going to do if I had received that piece of news. (Laughter)*
>
> *(...) The opposite of work is idleness. But very few of us know what to do with idleness. When you look at the way that we distribute our lives in general, you realize that in the periods in which we have a lot of money, we have very little time. And then when we finally*

have time, we have neither the money nor the health.

So, we started thinking about that as a company for the last 30 years. This is a complicated company with thousands of employees, hundreds of millions of dollars of business that makes rocket fuel propellent systems, runs 4,000 ATMs in Brazil, does income tax preparation for dozens of thousands. So, this is not a simple business.

And so, we said, look, the retirement, the whole issue of how we distribute our graph of life. Instead of going mountain climbing when you're 82, why don't you do it next week? And we'll do it like this, we'll sell you back your Wednesdays for 10 percent of your salary. So now, if you were going to be a violinist, which you probably weren't, you go and do this on Wednesday."[91]

Ricardo Semler does not empower. He **shares** Power. He has stripped away the blind authoritarianism that reduces Productivity. Workers are self-governing and self-managing.

Under the twenty years of his "Shapership™", Semco benefited from an exceptional growth rate, i.e., ten years after its transformation from an autocratic to a democratic structure, the company achieved 900 percent growth, productivity increased twofold despite severe economic recessions in Brazil, sales went from $11.000 per employee in 1979 to $135.000 in 1990's, more than four times what Semco's competitors achieve.

Ricardo Semler's innovative Business Management policies received a great deal of recognition all over the world.

---

[91] Ricardo Semler, How to run a company with (almost) no rules, TED talk 2014, https://www.ted.com/talks/ricardo_semler_how_to_run_a_company_with_almost_no_rules

He has managed to create a "Company Culture" based on people and not on his person, which makes Semco a unique model.

In addition to the many articles written about him, Ricardo Semler has transmitted his Leadership and Management experience in several books, some of which have been extremely successful.

In 1989 "Managing without Managers",

In 1993 "Maverick",

In 2002 "The seven-day weekend". (We offered this last book to several CEO's and are waiting for them to take a day off to read it!)

Is it possible that Ricardo Semler has been the Pioneer of the movement which generated a certain interest at the time and which lead to what is known today as the "Liberated Company"?

These models, published in popular books such as "Freedom Inc." [92] and "Reinventing organizations" [93] seem to find an important part of their inspiration in practices in which Ricardo Semler was a true Master: a maximum of both Focus and Freedom, Trust in Human Beings and the Art of challenging and taming one's own Ego.

---

[92] Freedom, INC.: Free Your Employees and Let Them Lead Your Business to Higher Productivity, Profits, and Growth, Brian M. Crney & Isaac Getz

[93] Reinventing organizations: a guide to creating organizations inspired by the next stage of Human Consciousness », Frederic Laloux

Michel Onfray (France, 1959-) - Shaper of Freedom of Thought through Philosophy

A well-known Philosopher, the son of a Norman farmer and a cleaning lady, he is the author of a considerable opus (more than 100 books), such as (our free adaptation of the titles in French)

- *The Art of enjoying. For a hedonistic materialism* (1991)
- *The Sculpture of the Self. The aesthetics ethics* (1993)
- *Appetites for thoughts. Philosophers and food (1995)*
- *Rebel politics. Treaty of Resistance and Insubordination* (1997)
- *Theory of the amorous body. For a Solar Erotic* (2000)
- "*Atheist Manifesto: The Case Against Christianity, Judaism and Islam*" (2005)
- his famous life opus, "*A Counter-History of Philosophy*"
- *A Hedonist Manifesto: The Power to Exist* (2006)
- a book on Freud published in 2010, "*The Twilight of an Idol: The Freudian Confabulation*", which has been the subject of considerable controversy in France because it "challenges" conventional ideas about Freud.
- The *Counter-History of Philosophy* which is already 11 volumes rich
- And a "*Counter-History of Literature*", whose first volume (2014) has a meaningful title considering "Shapership™": "*Le réel n'a pas eu lieu*"; literally, "*The Real did not happen*".

Abused by a compulsively violent mother who suffered herself from violence, Michel Onfray is abandoned in a catholic orphanage between age ten and fourteen, where he really discovers "hell": horror, violence, arbitrary authority and paedophilia.

And also, a "split" between "intellectual" and "manual" people which revolts him.

As he says, he "died at ten".

By the way, born in 1959, Michel Onfray almost died four times: the first time at twenty-eight from a Heart Attack and recently, in January 2018, from a cardiovascular arrest.

So, here is a man at the heart of Life, Matter, Body AND Spirit.

In fact, his re-education by a ruthless expert woman in Dietetics after his first AVC inspired his second book "*The belly of Philosophers: a critical approach to dietetics Reason*" (1989).

A book which creates a very contemporary link between Brain and Belly!

1. Creative Resistance: The Big "NO"

From the start, Michel Onfray is opposed to the conventional way Philosophy is taught in traditional Universities. He refuses to accept that there are subjects that are "philosophical" and others not! As he says,

> "There are only philosophical ways to approach any subject."

Between 1983 and 2002, he embodies his practices by being a Philosophy Teacher in a technical High School.

In 2002, shocked by the presence of a right-wing candidate in the second round of the French presidential election, Michel Onfray, who clearly carries very opposite values, has the feeling that the main reason why people adhere to the "extreme right" is because of a lack of collective Education in "Thinking".

2. The Transformative Vision: The Big "YES"

For him, "*Knowledge sets free, Ignorance enslaves*".

He promotes a teaching on the basis of which each one can build an "hedonistic" way of living.

It is an invitation for each person to think with an "Action Mind" and act in a thoughtful way.

Michel Onfray lives a **philosophical Life.**

He thinks Philosophy is not something you practice from 9:00 am to 5:00 pm. It is a 24/7 commitment.

He connects Head, Heart and Hands, which is typical of Shapers!

For him, probity and knowledge of the world are unavoidable keys:

> "*You must proceed from Reality and build upon it!*"

Of course, his approach is based on the **complete integration of the Lives and works of Philosophers** – the ones he studies and including himself - considering the connections between "Theory and Practice, between "Head, Heart and Hands" and how those dimensions can enlighten one another.

We might say that his own work and "Points of View" probably find an echo in the child abuse he experienced, in his fidelity to his social background and in a conviction that the "Mind" is not separated from the "Body".

For instance, *"The Counter History of Philosophy"* is designed to shed another light on Philosophers, by examining their Life and work, thus the inevitable imbrication between theory and practice. It either envisages philosophical works that are "neglected", forgotten - we could say *"mistreated"* -, or well-known masterpieces in an alternative way, in order to examine what they have to say that might have not been said before.

As another example: it is also meaningful that in the first volume of his *Counter History of Literature*, "*The Real did not happen*", he takes a never previously adopted point of view on the super famous Spanish Novel "Don Quixote", written by Cervantes in 1605.

"*The Real did not happen*" is a book on the denial of Reality.

Michel Onfray exposes two opposite characters

- Don Quixote who denies Reality (*what exists*) and "believes" that his own representations (Visions) are truer than what he "sees" (*what "Reality" shows*). His madness is that he does not want to see "*what is*" and prefers to see "*what he wants*"

- Sancho Panza who, like Saint Thomas, only believes in what he sees

It is interesting to note that Don Quixote believes in his "visions" in the exact opposite way Shapers do.

As Michel Onfray says,

> "*He does not believe what he sees but what he imagines. He imagines what he sees and believes it; what he believes becomes true and the "real" becomes a fiction. (...) He takes his desires for Reality.*"[94]

---

[94] Michel Onfray, Le Réel n'a pas eu Lieu. Le principe de Don Quichotte », Éditions Autrement, page 40

As you remember, Shapers see *"What is"* AND *"What could be"*.

Not one nor the other.

It is also because they are in close connection with the "real" that they can feel what the world needs and can develop a Transformative Vision.

That is what Michel Onfray wants to do, to be and to transmit, with his "Body of Knowledge".

Of course, he often challenges the dogmas created by traditional institutions and people.

He disturbs! He upsets!

3. Anticipative Experimentation: L'Université Populaire de Caen

In 2002, witnessing the rise of the right-wing political candidates, he engages his philosophical life in a new direction.

He resigns from the National Education Administration and, with a group of friends, creates "L'Université Populaire" in Caen, which gives everyone free access to lectures on Philosophy and others cultural fields.

This fits perfectly with the heritage of Condorcet i.e. *"Obtain from public power an instruction which makes Reason popular"*.

> « *L'Université Populaire is not Victor Cousin's University!*
> *As a matter of fact, it is nobody's University!*
> *It does not depend on any guardian authority under the light of which it would be wise to be situated, because shadows make the enemies of Light happy.*

It is an open society, a centrifugal system,

One could adopt the exact opposite definition of the institutional University to propose that of the Popular University: it has noticed the Relativism suggested by Nietzsche, it thinks under the light of History, it cares about what is concrete, about the Earth, about the solid material, it acts in untimely ways, it is satisfied with the given world, it decides free from any political centre, therefore it does not reject anything at the margins, it places existential edification at the forefront of its preoccupations, it clearly claims democratic exoterism; it does not assess anything or anyone, leaving everyone the option to choose the way to Wisdom at one's own pace; it teaches interacting between Life and the Opus, the necessary imbrication of Theory and Practice, the implication of the body in the making of a Reason; it does not wish to develop a brigade of civil servants but rather to generate a community of friends; it spares neither Society, nor the State, nor Power, nor Religions!

(...)

In what ways does it generate effects?
Through the freedom of entering or exiting this open system, through friendly co-optation, by the shared denial to believe that there are certain subjects which are philosophical and others which are not, by showing that ways to approach any subject or topic are always philosophical. (...)

The denial of "Philosophia Perennis" highly respected by the Institutional University and the installation "in the field", not of a specifically philosophical subject but of a philosophical treatment of any possible subject, opens our Caen "approach" to Cinema, Psycho analysis, Contemporary Art, Feminism, Gender Studies, Philosophy for children, Jazz, Bioethics, Contemporary Literature, Architecture, Musicology, Classical Music, Political Ideas, Readings of great Philosophical texts, History and Literary Eroticism.

Without forgetting the Popular University of Taste in Argentan, offering a philosophical approach of the 5 senses – Cinema and Contemporary Art, Music and Gastronomy, Cooking and Philosophy for Children.
*"The Popular University is not the Liberal response to the increasing contemporary demand for Philosophy, nor a cash-generating machine, a theoretical club, a University for the working class, a Marxist school not even a centralized jacobine institution. Rather, it is an epicurean creation, a community of friends sharing the same desire: **make a revolution without gaining Power**".*[95]

The tuition-free "Université Populaire" generates an enormous interest. Each course attracts hundreds of people each week. They are broadcasted on the France Culture radio station and reach a massive audience, using podcasts and CD packs they generate.

Michel Onfray's intention, which is clearly one of a left-wing man, never aims at lowering levels – especially his, which is brilliant – but to raise the spirit and the mind of others towards higher Knowledge, a broadened and freer

---

[95] Michel Onfray, Rendre la raison populaire, Éditions Autrement, 2012

way to think, thus towards more Freedom and more conscious Choices.

His proposals obviously don't remain theoretical and also include the "body". It is the case of the Popular University of Taste, founded in 2006, the initial purpose of which is to propose Education to Gastronomy.

Among other goals, it allows people with limited financial means to discover healthy, affordable and delicious ways to feed themselves. Rather than buying tasteless and expensive products in supermarkets, people learn to buy, to cook and enjoy products, wines and products – which are better, local, more authentic. Another fight against ignorance and fatalisation.

His heritage goes far beyond the philosophical content he transmits and beyond his capacity to "offer" to numerous people - of all ages, social and cultural backgrounds - access to Philosophy.

He decided to live a philosophical Life - Body, Mind and Soul - so his Life is his heritage.

He lives in his Integrity and in his Coherence between his Life and his work.

One might like him or not, agree or disagree with him but it takes an enormous amount of courage to speak, not "the" Truth, but "one's" Truth and, if only for that, he might be considered as a source of inspiration and someone who makes the world a better place.

Rob Hopkins (United Kingdom, 1968-) - Shaper of the Transition Culture Movement

Rob Hopkins was born is Chiswick, England and today, lives in Totnes, a city he made famous by making it the first "Transition Town" in the world!

Rob Hopkins grew up in London. He studied on England's south coast and holds a master's in Human and Social Sciences and a Doctorate from Plymouth University.

He also travelled the world and obviously deepened some spiritual matters! At age twenty, he spends two years in a Tibetan Buddhist temple in Tuscany as House Manager. He then spent a year in India, in Pakistan, in China, in Tibet and in Hong Kong

Since 1996, his life is one of a writer, educator and militant in Ecology. At any rate, it is the life of a man who practices what he preaches. While living in Ireland with his family, he worked on an ecovillage project, bought a farm with another family, and started teaching Permaculture in 2001, first over a one-year cycle in a college in Ireland then on a two-year cycle all over the world.

His life is based on many years of experience in Education, teaching people practical skills for Sustainability such as Permaculture and Natural Building.

In 2012, he was voted one of the top 100 environmentalists and was on Nesta and the Observer's list of Britain Fifty New radicals.

1. Creative Resistance: The Big "NO".

> In 2004, he becomes acutely aware of one of the great challenges of our time: oil peak and the necessity for all of us to radically change the way we live and engage in a Transition.

Simultaneously, his background makes him particularly aware of the incapacity of current institutions to give a pertinent response to this challenge.

2. The Transformative Vision: The Big "YES".

He develops the conviction that what is needed, above all else, at this time in History, is "***Engaged Optimism***": a transformation by and for the people.

He has a Vision of a radically hopeful Community-driven approach to creating resilient Societies independent from fossil fuels.

As Rob Hopkins says,

> "*What would it look like if the best responses to peak oil and climate change came not from committees and Acts of Parliament, but from you and me and the people around us?*" [96]

His concept is called "Transition Initiatives":

> "*A place where there is a community-led process that helps a town/village/ city/ neighbourhood become stronger and happier*".

So, here is a vision of local communities, connected by a sense of a "place" they belong to and care for, actively engaged in re-imagining their own Future, designing ways to leverage local cooperation and interdependence to shrink their ecological footprint, to prepare for a "Post Oil Future" and move from Oil dependence to local resilience.

The "Transition Response" is really about looking at the challenges of peak oil and climate change square in the

---

[96] The Transition Companion, Making your community more resilient in uncertain times, Rob Hopkins

face and responding with all the Creativity, Imagination and Adaptability needed.

It is a sort of "Power-to-the-People" approach: the sustainable Future of a local community is co-created in a collaborative process by and for the everyday people of that community, who at the same time are participating in finding "local solutions to global problems".

3. Anticipative Experimentation: The co-creation of local responses to global problems by people for people

In 2005, he settles in Totnes, England and, transforming his Vision into Action, he starts a pioneering experiment: "Transition Town Totnes", the first city in official transition.

A group of committed citizens engages in a self-organized and collective intelligence exercise, to envision viable possible paths towards a new and vibrant Future they can create for themselves.

The citizens are not only discussing, thinking and dreaming; they also connect with the local community, look for ways to make localization a Reality on the ground, e.g. through local food projects, Community supported Agriculture schemes, Community-owned Energy companies, alternative currencies and Energy descent plans.

« Totnes, Transition Town » is an expansion –not a dispersion- of self-organized projects: Keeping Totnes Warm, Open Eco Homes and Eco Homes Fair, Transition Homes, Transition Streets (which is rewarded by the Ashden price in 2011 changes in Behaviours), Totnes & District Energy Descent action plan, Totnes Economic Centre, The Local Entrepreneurs Forum, The Totnes

Pound, Totnes Transition Film Festival, TTT film Club, le TTT Film Club, Dr. Bike, Caring Town Totnes et Transition Tours.

Rob Hopkins shares everything: his Vision, his knowledge, methods, tools in two books *"The Transition Handbook: from oil dependence to local resilience"* (2008) and *"The Transition Companion: making your community more resilient in uncertain times"* (2011). Rob Hopkins has also created various blogs.

All this inspires and supports the Transition Network which he co-founded in 2007 to assist the numerous Transition initiatives emerging all over the world.

A Movement is born.

Hundreds of similar communities have sprung up around the world.

Twelve years after its creation, the Movement has swarmed in over fifty countries and 1.500 groups are officially identified on the website.

The "Transition Initiatives" answer a growing collective Shift in Awareness, not only from Totnes people, but from the entire world. Deep down, people know that "Business as Usual" is not an answer if we are to have a Future on this Planet.

There is a need to find new ways forward.

People also have an inner feeling that it is time to stop the story of "somebody else is going to do it for us!". They feel that, although the Transition movement is not going to solve all the issues, it is "historic landmark: now is the time and the opportunity to do something useful!

People are also rediscovering common connections and recognizing more and more that local solutions can emerge from their own shared will, commitment, collaborative power and action. Transition Town not only resonates with their deepest and untapped aspirations; it shows them a path to the Future and a way to "craft" it together.

Today, Rob Hopkins is presented as the initiator in 2005 of the International Transition Towns Movement, which, of course is an "hindsight" type of interpretation.

Rob Hopkins did not start as a Leader. He started as a Shaper in his own town, probably without making any specific plans on what was going to follow! He said a Big NO to one situation, a Big YES to Transition by the people for the people and a historical moment developed without turning him into a leader or an entrepreneur!

Just a Shaper. A man who sees that the "Possible" is richer than the "Real", who inspires new visions and new actions to make the world a better place.

It is this precise articulation between the clarity of his "NO" and the optimism of his "YES" that makes Rob Hopkins such an "Eye Opener" and a "High Opener"! Rather than reinforcing fear or despair, he creates a strong desire for a Future in which Imagination plays a fundamental role. It is the famous "believe so you can see» of the Shaper busy giving form to the Future instead of the current "see first and then believe".

In a 2018 article [97], he declares:

> « I am often told that Transition will never work unless we attack Capitalism first! I think this is a form of denial, of excuse to do nothing. What can I do to destroy or change Capitalism from my home, in my town? If you take this massive objective and break it into a multitude

---

[97] https://usbeketrica.com/article/rob-hopkins-transition-capitalisme-alternative, in French, free translation by us

of smaller tasks, there are many of these little tasks that can be done locally.

Maybe we can create our own banks; maybe we can boost our local and independent Economy; help the farms in our Community to grow; make sure the money stays where we live rather than go to multinational companies which in turn will place them in Tax havens.

For me, we can start undermining Capitalism by opposing an attractive alternative, something that offers more than Capitalism does! Capitalism generates Solitude, Social Isolation, Misery and Anxiety. To replace it, we can generate projects which link people together, generate new jobs, allow the placement of money in other places, give access to better and affordable food.

To me THAT is the answer to Capitalism!

Imagination plays a key role in guiding our reactions! (...)

The words we place at the centre of any conversation have an important impact. If you place Despair, Collapse and say that we are too late, this totally paralyzes any conversation and it becomes very difficult to be creative and imaginative!

There is a lot of despair nowadays, and very justified it is too! It is difficult not to despair when you read or hear the news about the climate. But if we are too late, it means that all is left for us to do is to manage the overall disintegration. And the best way to manage the situation is to be imaginative! There is always an opportunity to bypass the worst. The GIEC tells us that we must reinvent everything and that requires a collective effort of Imagination.

Much too often, people who fight against that put Dystopia at the centre of the room. But who wants to hear that? I'd rather have you help me imagine what another world might look like!
To my mind, what mobilizes people is a story about the Future which is still possible to invent.
That Future may entail of certain amount of collapse, but we must talk about it in a delicious and exciting way. We must give people things they yearn for."

He develops this further in his book "From what is to what if!", published in 2019.

Thanks to his intuition of what is possible, to his example and inspiration, Rob Hopkins succeeded in making millions of people change their ways of Seeing, Thinking and Acting, independently of any central organization imposing a model.

It is certainly not the first attempt to create a way of life which completely fits with the needed "transition". But thanks to the timing, the way of operating and sharing, and many other factors, Transition has now become a self-appropriated concept, thus a Movement.

An Open Source, viral, self-emergent and self-organizing Movement of enthused Shapers of local communities, committed to give Transition a "go", gathering in an informal way but clearly walking the trails their friends of Totness blazed, to find specific local solutions as well as exchanging learnings from their experimentations around the world.

THE ART OF SHAPERSHIP

The Transition Movement initiated by Rob Hopkins is simply irreversible. Nicholas Crane, presenter of BBC2's "Town series", referred to Transition as

> *"The biggest urban brainwave of the century".*

It has now become a "Transition Culture". The baseline they chose – *"An evolving exploration into the head, heart and hands of energy descent"* - clearly states the specific way Shapers "craft" Reality thanks to the connections between these dimensions. It also illustrates the will to adopt an Altitude Attitude which permanently connects Vision and Action.

Chapter 7

Some emerging and potential Shapers

Vishen Lakhiani (Malaysia, United States, 1976-) - Shaper of Self-Development for all

If we had to place Vishen into known categories, we could say he is

- a real entrepreneur - he has founded three companies – one of which is Mindvalley, an Education Technology company focused on Spiritual Development and Lifelong Learning and, by the way, one of the fastest growing companies in the world

- an **author**: he published "The Code of the extraordinary Mind". After its publication in May 2016, the book reached #10 on the New York Times Bestseller list for Advice, How-to & Miscellaneous

- an inspiring **speaker** on Conscious Entrepreneurship and Company Culture

- an **"educator"**: his speeches are designed as guidance and the events he creates are "training" opportunities

THE ART OF SHAPERSHIP

He could well become the Shaper of Self-Development for all.

He has this capacity to radically challenge the status quo, to sense what the world needs.

He also embodies the type of bold BIG Yesses that Shapers dare to think about.

As Elon Musk, who he recognizes as one of his sources of Inspiration, he might be considered among

> "Individuals with outsized dreams"[98]

But it did not start like that.

Born in Kuala Lumpur, Malaysia, he grows up in what he calls the "developing world", in a family where his mother is a public-school teacher and his dad a hard-working entrepreneur, running an export/import company.

He moves to the United States and studies Computer Engineering at the University of Michigan because, as he says

> "In the 1990's every Indian family wanted their son to be the next Bill Gates. He was the richest man in the world. I studied computer engineering because, you know, kind of it was what my society expected me to do, not because I really enjoyed it."

In 1998, he graduates with low grades – he considers himself as a bad engineer – and he ends up obtaining an internship at Microsoft.

In the United States, he discovers and becomes an Active member of AIESEC, a non-for-profit organization which encourages young students in Economics to grow and to make a difference in the world.

---

[98] https://mixergy.com/interviews/vishen-lakhiani-MindValley-interview/

Vishen considers that growing up in Malaysia *"made me grow up with mediocre dreams."*

> *"My vision of the world was what I saw around me. And that vision was mediocre. I saw engineers working in Gray-walled factories supervising factory workers in assembly plants. That was my vision of what it was to be an entrepreneur, to be an engineer.*
> *In terms of entrepreneurship, I mean, my Dad was my "entrepreneuring" role model. He inspired me to be an entrepreneur but the way he worked in terms of entrepreneurship and what I witnessed wasn't very attractive. So, growing up in the developing world, the big issue is you don't dream nearly big enough. Now, the internet is changing that. During the Nineties, when I was a teenager, that was what I saw. So, my whole vision of the world in business was kind of grey compared to what we see now."*

Inspired by the tons of books and biographies he reads, he finds inspiration and hope in the story of Akio Morita, who founded Sony in what Vishen considers a "worse climate" than his own: post-war Japan.

All this, plus his studies in the United-States and the time he spent at Microsoft

> *"...set a new benchmark for who I wanted to be as an entrepreneur. I decided I wanted to give my employees flexitime. I wanted office beer keg parties on Fridays. I wanted to be able to take my employees, put them in a bus, ship them out to movies, all of this changed that view."*

After he gets fired from Microsoft - when they discover how bad an engineer he is – the only job he can get with his low grades is for a non-for-profit organization in New-York, below the poverty line. He then moves to Silicon Valley. The first two companies he starts go bust.

Now, he is completely broke.

He then gets a job as a Technology salesman, paid on commission with no base salary.

He makes two dollars the first month.

Highly stressed by his situation, he takes a class on Meditation.

> *"A crazy thing happened. After that class my performance improved so much, I got promoted three times in four months and they made me Director of Sales. They shipped me out to New York. So, there I was, this 27-year-old Malaysian kid now running the company's entire New York office. I continued my Meditation practice and I decided to become certified, so I could teach it and really master it, right? Because the best way to learn is to teach.*
> *That's where my computer engineering skills came back, and I could build a website program, and start my own little website to teach Meditation. That business, which I started for $700 dollars grew into what MindValley is today. Within one year after starting, I quit my job and dedicated myself full time to MindValley and, you know, it's grown into the company that it is today."*

Mindvalley, which he co-founded at 26, in Times Square, New York before settling it in Kuala Lumpur, has become an Education Technology company focused on Spiritual Development and Lifelong Learning.

Funnily enough, Vishen is *"a guy who called himself a mediocre entrepreneur, who previously got shot down when he tried to get funding, and yet he took $700, only $700, and built a company that's now valued at over $40 million.*[99]

Here is his Big "NO"

"And so, the whole reason I run MindValley, is to hack Education and get out to the world, the kind of Education I wished I got when I was a teenager."

Now his Big "YES".

MindValley's purpose is no less than **"Pushing Humanity forward"**.

"Our goal is to help spread enlightened ideas to 1 billion people by 2050, ideas that you won't get from traditional Education systems."

"I like simplicity, and in my first two businesses, I wrote very detailed business plans, right? Complete failure. The way I approach things right now is it all starts with a vision in my head.

Now, it's a vision of like, you know, what do I want to build? It's not, it's never for the money, I'm always driven by wanting to make deep change, and in my case, what really drives me, is wanting to get out to people embodiment practices, such as mindfulness, gratitude,

---

[99] https://mixergy.com/interviews/vishen-lakhiani-MindValley-interview/

> *exercise, fitness. I'm crazy about how I treat my mind and my body. And I believe that there's so much missing in Education."*

Here is the Creative Experimentation: The Creative "HOW"

His company is pioneering a completely new type of publishing focused on spiritual development.

How do they succeed?

Through Culture-Hacking Communities and revolutionizing the Global Education System.

They have super products and are super focused on outcomes, i.e. the Value they can bring to people's life. For instance

> *"We have close to a 42-point checklist. It's very, very detailed based on how we've developed as a company. There are a lot of different factors. I'd say the most important thing is we start with the end in mind, which is Transformation. What is it going to do to a person's life, whether it's their physique, or their health, or their state of mind, 30 days from using this product?"*

The first MindValley Mobile application is "OmVana", a beautiful Meditation and concentration app. (It was presented at CBS news and entrepreneurs.com)

> *"Within five months of launching Omvana, by applying conversion hacking, we managed to get Omvana onto the number one, highest grossing app for health and fitness, in 24 countries.*

> *Our forte was not so much creating information products. Our forte was really the conversion, the converting of it. How to create an entire ecosystem where you can put up ads in Google, get people to come to a page, sign up for free content or demo content, and then from there get them to invest in a full-fledged product."*

Being a Shaper is also keeping this capacity to connect, create synergies, across fields, beyond divisions of all sorts and to create a "Mayonnaise": a whole which is more than the sum of the parts.

For instance, OmVana combines and leverages three different assets the company has developed:

- access to hundreds of authors thanks to their publishing division,
- mobile app development know-how
- design skills

Vishen has developed a vision of Leadership – No! He doesn't talk about Shapership™ yet – which is:

> *"Recognizing that every individual has within him/her the power to be as powerful, influential, brilliant and magnificent as the leader and helping each person remember and unleash that power."*

Now here is a terrific illustration of the famous saying **"the Eye only sees what the Brain is ready to understand"!**

Look at what happened between year Five and six of MindValley's existence:

> "In year five, May 2008, Mike and I realized that even though we were making about a quarter million dollars a month, we were actually losing $15 grand a month. We were burning more money than we were actually pulling in and we knew that if this continued, we were going to end up having to lay off employees. We had 18 employees back then.
>
> Now, 8 months later, the business had gone through a massive transformation. It grew 400% between May 2008 and December 2008."

What happened?

Vishen rewired his Brain.

He realized what we said at the beginning of this book: "It is our mind that creates our reality, not the opposite."

He realized he had belief systems that were creating his current Reality.

Here are extracts of an interview he gave that illustrate, in his own words, his vision and how he embodies it.

> "A lot of people think the way to become successful in business is to learn the next trick. And by trick, I mean, it's this new book on Culture or this new thing about Strategy. Measuring KPI's. Right?
>
> Ultimately, what I've recognized is that it's all about two things, and the two things are as follows.
>
> **Number one.** It's your models of Reality. It's your models of the world. Now, when you start meditating, you go into a very introspective state of mind.

Especially when you're combining Meditation with reading autobiographies and books. By monitoring your own thoughts, you become acutely aware of your own beliefs and whether those beliefs serve you or not.
So, you start to recognize your models of the world that no longer work.

I started identifying my beliefs. It's crazy. You start seeing your thought process. I began to realize that I had issues with money. Money made me feel guilty. I began to understand that I had belief patterns that I inherited as a child.

For example, I believed that I had to work my butt off to be wealthy. And if I wanted to cut back working hours so I could spend more time with my one-year old son Hayden, well then, I was going to have to postpone success. That's what I actually believed back then. It sounds so stupid. But that was my belief. And many of us have these beliefs that we don't realize we have.

Now, that was what we call the "Success Comes from Hard Work Rule". Absolute bullshit. We now call those rules Bullshit Rules that govern how we view the world.

Now once I was able to flip out those belief patterns, I was able to actually see changes in my physical reality and in my business.

I realized I could work the same hours but make massively more. In eight months, we grew revenues 400 percent. But here's the cool thing, right? One year after this big shift, I only spent six days in the office, 21 days on beaches around the world. And in that month, we had our biggest ever revenue month and our single biggest sales day. Now, what happened?

When you switch your belief system, it's like you swoosh away your brain works.

You start identifying and looking at things in a different way.

Our beliefs change the way we react with the world, the way we observe the world.

And what happened when I got rid of these belief systems is that I stopped buying into my own bullshit excuses. I stopped.

When I was able to see that these were nothing more than beliefs and I could choose to accept them or ignore them, I realized could create my own reality.

That's what I started doing.

The second thing *is that what really defines you as a human being are your systems, the things you do on a daily basis that govern how you work.*

Yet, we don't think about the systems of our consciousness.

Now there are many things that scientists say that you can do on a daily basis that completely change your consciousness. Things, for example, such as Gratitude. I mean, do you know that there are studies that show that just applying Gratitude to your life can boost your Happiness levels considerably? And I mean massively. Massive boost in Happiness.

Or Meditation can change the way you see yourself. Or visualizing your goals can help you make them come true. ***Now if you asked me what's the secret,*** *I've got to say it's being able to be acutely aware of the models in my head and to remove the beliefs that no longer serve me. And then visualizing every single day how I want my Life to unfold three years from now, and how I want my day to unfold so that three-year vision becomes a reality."* [100]

The company's Management is well balanced and based on those two elements so often mentioned by Shapers:

- **a maximum of Focus**: a team of more than 100 people from over thirty countries focused on building disruptive systems that push Humanity forward
- **and a maximum of Freedom**: in 2012, MindValley's Headquarters, which is designed to foster Happiness, Creativity and Productivity was rewarded by Inc. Magazine readers as one of the World's Coolest Offices.

MindValley's work Culture has received the award for Most Democratic Workplace for five years in a row and, in April 2014, MindValley was listed among the forty-one companies in the world certified for their democratic organizational design.

Vishen has also launched other Wealth-creating initiatives such as:

- the MindValley Academy: an online University dedicated to Personal development
- Project Renaissance

---

[100] https://mixergy.com/interviews/vishen-lakhiani-MindValley-interview/

- the Awesomeness Festival, a non-for-profit and invite-only conference which gathers entrepreneurs, authors, artists, visionaries and offers transformational training in conscious entrepreneurship and Mindfulness

As other Shapers, he has a long-term Vision and an **Ecosystem Strategy**.

> "You don't just build one Business. You build one Business, but you use it as a launch pad to launch a second Business. I look at the assets that we have right now. The assets are current Businesses that we have right now, and I figure out how to connect these assets to launch a completely new Business."

He is also member of the Innovation Board of the XPRIZE Foundation and, with other philanthropist, he helps the organization to define their annual Big Challenges. He is in Tune with the world.

In 2015, at XPRIZE's Visioneering Event, he was part of the team that won the audience vote for best new XPRIZE Idea called "Human Dignity X PRIZE".

It was dedicated to revolutionizing housing for refugees thanks to radical cost reduction and in increased durability.

They invented *"inexpensive, deployable in a day, safe/secure homes with access to water, sanitation, and off-the-grid power, for displaced families that can be integrated to create more than just shelters and provide the development of communities created by those who live in them"*[101]

So again, a Big "NO": a major challenge to a situation considered as Unacceptable and a Big "Yes":

---

[101] http://labs.blogs.com/its_alive_in_the_lab/2015/05/autodesk-participation-in-xprize-visioneering-1st-place-for-a-2nd-time.html

> "*Even though they can't go home, they can be at home*".

In 2017, he was awarded winner of "Most Strategic Entrepreneur" in SME & Entrepreneurship Business Award, Malaysia 2017.

He has now become a source of inspiration in his own developing country and can help people "dream Big".

Salman Khan (Bengal, United States, 1976 -) - "Shaper of Education for Many".

Salman Khan is a brilliant man who received a high-level Education. He holds three diplomas from MIT and an MBA from Harvard Business School.

He is the founder of the Kahn Academy, a non-profit educational website created in 2006 which uses video to reinvent Education.

His ambition is clear: « Provide high-level teaching to everyone, everywhere".

It all started in 2004 with lessons in Mathematics that Salman gave to his niece Nadia. Salman offered her small tutorials he conceived thanks to Yahoo's Doodle Notes. Considering the success of these tutorials with parents and friends of his niece, Salman decided to put his tutorials on You Tube.

Each tutorial is a mini lesson about ten minutes long, during which his face does not appear, but his voice is heard. They are filmed as if Salman were sitting by the side of the student working on a problem on a sheet of paper. Each lesson includes a blackboard on the computer screen on which Salman draws while explaining vocally how he solves the problem.

Considering the popularity and the success of his tutorials, Salman Khan leaves his job in Finance in 2009 to dedicate himself fulltime to the Kahn Academy.

As of December 2009, Khan's tutorials hosted on You Tube get an average of 35000 hits per day!

Kahn Academy proposes a carefully structured series of educational video tutorials offering complete curricula in Mathematics, Astronomy, Physics, Cosmology, Organic Chemistry, Medicine, Biology, and more.

All resources are available for free to anyone around the world.

The website publishes online a free library of more than 2200 mini-lessons. Offline versions of the videos have been distributed by associations in rural areas in Asia, Latin America and Africa, thus allowing teachers and students to access a totally new form of learning.

The model eliminates economic barriers that prevent effective Education, as long as an individual has regular access to an internet enabled computer.

Salman Khan's long-term objective is to supply tens of thousands of videos on almost every possible topic and subject and to create the first worldwide free virtual school.

Today, Khan Academy has eclipsed MIT Open CourseWare in terms of videos viewed.

Its YouTube channel has more than 400 million total views, compared to MIT's fifty-eight million.

It reaches about 10,000,000 students per month and has delivered over 300,000,000 lessons.

The continuously improving system also provides online exercises adapted to the level of competence and performance of the students. Soon, it will probably make it possible to personalize Teaching and make it collaborative.

Salman Khan thinks that his academy demonstrates the possibility to reconsider the paradigm of the traditional classroom, and facts seem to indicate he is right!

THE ART OF SHAPERSHIP

Jack Andraka (United States, 1997 -) - Shaper of a new system for cancer detection

Jack Andraka was born on January 8th, 1997 in the state of Maryland.

In 2012, at age fifteen, he invents a low-cost and very fast method for early detection of pancreatic cancer.

In 2013, the scientific Press stresses the fact that his project is

> (...)168 times faster, 26.000 times less expensive and 400 times more sensitive than the current tests present on the market.

> Jack Andraka even thinks his test could be used to detect ovary and lung cancers, and that by simply changing the protein the test reacts to, it could even allow to diagnose other diseases such as heart diseases and even AIDS!

> This invention is the reason why he received the first prize at the Intel International Science and Engineering Fair (Intel ISEF). And, cherry on the cake, added to the satisfaction of having contributed to the progress of research, he also received a 75.000-dollar check. [102]

Even if the efficiency of his scientific discovery has since then been challenged by some, his approach and his story are those of a Shaper and may inspire others.

---

[102] https://www.20minutes.fr/sciences/1110869-20130301-etats-unis-15-ans-invente-outil-depistage-cancer-pancreas

1. Creative Resistance: The Big "NO"

At age thirteen, Jack experiences a painful loss: a close family friend he considered as his uncle dies from pancreatic cancer with metastasis. Under shock, Jack wants to know more.

He surfs on the Internet and what he discovers shocks him even more: over 85 percent of pancreatic cancers are diagnosed too late, when a person has less than 2 percent chances to survive.

Why? Because screening tests are expensive, hence rarely prescribed by physicians. Moreover, they lack precision and only detect 30 percent of pancreatic cancers.

2. Transformative Vision: The Big "YES"

At that very moment, what started due a personal pain gets transformed into a project which, potentially, answers the needs of millions of people.

Jack sets himself a mission: invent an early screening test for pancreatic cancer. But, since he wants to have a radical impact, he sets himself scientific criteria: his system must be low-cost, fast, simple, sharp, selective and minimally invasive.

3. Anticipative Experimentation

Jack continues his investigations on the Internet and, as he puts it: "I connected myself to the Teenagers" two best friends i.e. Google and Wikipedia. I used them all the time to do my homework".

At one point, he discovers an article which lists over 8.000 different proteins that can be found when someone has pancreatic cancer.

He then decides to go over these 8.000 proteins and to identify a "marker" of that type of cancer which can be found in large quantities in every patient, even those diagnosed early.

Driven by what he calls a "teenager enthusiasm", closer to Faith than anything else, he begins to test the 8.000 proteins. At the 4000th test, close to getting mad, he discovers what he was looking for!

> *"The protein I had identified was called Mesothelin. It is a simple, even banal type of protein, unless you are attacked by pancreatic, ovary or lung cancer, in which cases large quantities of it can be found in the blood system. The essential element being that it can be found at the early stage of the disease when the person has 100% chances to survive. Now that I had found a reliable and detectable protein, I changed my approach in order to detect it and hence detect pancreatic cancer."*

During one of his Biology classes on antibodies and while he is discreetly reading an article on carbon Nano tubes, the idea hits him that it would be possible to associate both and to manufacture a paper-based blood test.

> *"Producing a cancer detector with paper is almost as simple as making chocolate cookies, which I crave. You take water, you pour it into the nanotubes, you add the antibodies and you mix. Take the paper, dip it, dry it and you are able to detect a cancer."*

Is it possible to think in such a simple way when one's brain is filled with Knowledge or it this the privilege of a young mind?

At this stage, Jack has a problem imagining going on with his research on cancer in his mother's kitchen! He decides to pursue his work in a laboratory.

His words best express what happens next!

> *« So, I typed up a budget, a supply and equipment list, a timeline, and a procedure, and I emailed it to 200 different professors at Johns-Hopkins University and the National Institutes of Health -- essentially, anyone that had anything to do with pancreatic cancer. I sat back waiting for these positive emails to be pouring in, saying, "You're a genius! You're going to save us all!"*

Over the course of a month, he receives 199 NO's out of those 200 emails.

And it is not just about 199 refusals of his idea of developing a test to detect pancreatic cancer; some professors even take time to demolish his idea and to explain why it is a lousy one!

Fortunately, one professor agrees to open the doors of his laboratory: Dr Anirban Maitra, Professor of Oncology and biomolecular Engineering at the prestigious Johns-Hopkins University in Baltimore.

Three months later, he has his own laboratory! Assisted by other scientists, he works very hard during the next seven months in order to make his test stronger.

The result is a small paper detector allowing for a non-invasive test, lasting five minutes and costing three cents!!! In other words, 168 times faster, over 26.000 cheaper and over 400 times more precise than existing systems at the time. Moreover, it allows to detect cancers earlier than other methods.

During the preliminary testing period, the system presents 100 percent reliability.

Moreover, since the test also measures the level of Mesothelin in the patient's blood, and since this protein is also present in lung and ovary cancers, the new test could be used for several types of screenings.

As Dr. Anirban Maitra (of Johns-Hopkins University) who gave Jack his chance says:

> *"This kid is the Edison of our times. There are going to be a lot of light bulbs coming from him!"*
>
> (The Baltimore Sun 5/24/2012)

How great for Jack when you think his idea had been refused by 199 laboratories!

How lucky for Jack to have had this curious mind and access - through Internet - to the type of knowledge he needed to continue.

How wonderful that he was so Enthusiasm and Faith-driven to pursue his work, in spite of difficulties, rejection and criticisms, some of them coming from so-called "authorities" in the field!

How amazing he had the intelligence and the "freshness" to "pivot" several times during his research!

Finally, how fortunate for the world that he did not stop because of preconceived ideas about himself – young age, lack of knowledge in the field – in short that he did not take "Reality" as an excuse NOT TO DO!

Maybe, as certain critics say, his « test » is not perfect!

What is remarkable is that Jack opened new trails and new hopes and not only from a scientific viewpoint.

His whole attitude opens a reflexion at the very heart of Shapership™: in our hyper connected world, no "title" and no "position" are required to have an impact!

> *"And so, hopefully one day, we can all have that one extra uncle, that one mother, that one brother, sister, we can have that one more family member to love. And that one day, our hearts will be rid of that one disease burden that comes from pancreatic, ovarian and lung cancer, and potentially any disease. But through the Internet, anything is possible.*
>
> *Theories can be shared, and you don't have to be a professor with multiple degrees to have your ideas valued. It's a neutral space, where what you look like, age or gender -- doesn't matter.*
>
> *It's just your ideas that count.*
>
> *For me, it's all about looking at the Internet in an entirely new way, to realize that there's so much more to it than just posting duck-face pictures of yourself online. (Laughter) You could be changing the world. So, if a 15-year old who didn't even know what a pancreas was could find a new way to detect pancreatic cancer -- just imagine what you could do.* [103]"

---

[103] http://www.ted.com/talks/jack_andraka_a_promising_test_for_pancreatic_cancer_from_a_teenager?language=fr

The case of Elon Musk
(South Africa, United States, 1971 -)

Is he a Shaper?

And if not, why?

His name is famous. He even made the cover of Time magazine.

He is considered by some young people as an idol.

He is hated by others.

On Wikipedia, far from being described as a Shaper, the first sentence of his profile says:

> "Elon Reeve Musk is a South African-born American business magnate, investor and engineer".

Then follows the impressive list of initiatives he launched.

It is difficult to refrain a "Wow" of some sort, isn't?

Why? Because they are extra-ordinary. Not ordinary.

Ambitious. Bold, some might say.

So, we decided to look at him with the "Shaper's lens".

Beyond the facts related to his life, what can we find that would give us this perspective on him?

1. Creative Resistance: The Big "NO"

> When we talk about Creative Resistance as a way to look at Reality as it is and say a big No to a taken-for-granted situation, Elon Musk matches the criteria.

He certainly is the type of person who is permanently dissatisfied with the way things are.

He is a super challenger of the status quo.

He is also super gifted for sensing what is called a "demand": a space for transformative Innovation and impact. A place where deep needs exist to significantly improve people's lives.

For instance, he looks at the way Mobility is currently managed and finds that the current approaches and practices need to be radically challenged.

He looks at payment systems and questions the way they operate.

He looks at the threats on the Future of Humanity and challenges our capacity to have any future on this planet.

He looks at rocket science and says:

> " *Rocket technology had not materially improved since the '60s—arguably it had gone backward! We decided to reverse that trend.*[104]"

He looks at the type of solutions we find to issues - placed in neatly separated boxes - and he connects them!

He is definitely not chained in the prison of facts or representations.

2. Transformative Vision: The Big "YES"

Elon Musk does not spend much time criticizing.

He moves forward with his creative reconstruction of Reality.

---

[104] https://www.wired.com/2012/10/ff-elon-musk-qa/all/

He excels at formulating short and bold "Visions" of "What could be".

- He doesn't say he is going to improve Mobility; he sets himself the goal to "Catalyse Sustainable Mobility". That's Tesla!

- He doesn't say he is going to reduce the costs of sending satellite carrying rockets; he sets himself the goal to radically decrease their cost. The result: a launch at 1/10 of those costs while maintaining a 70 percent Growth margin. That's Space X!

- He doesn't say that we should diminish our CO2 imprints or better manage natural resources to reduce the ecological risks Humanity faces – which in fact is simply Extinction; he says,

    "Sooner or later, we must expand Life beyond this green and blue ball—or go extinct."

    "I want to die on Mars, but not on landing"

    So, he wants to perpetuate the human race by colonizing Mars in case of major threats to Humanity on Earth. Space X long-term purpose is "creating a true space-faring civilization".

- About transportation of people and goods between cities, he doesn't say he is going to build faster cars, bigger trucks or faster airplanes; he decides to dig two parallel tunnels between two cities where pressurized trains will travel at 900 km/h. That's the Future of high-speed travel, "Hyper Loop", developed by the Boring company. [105]

Who else would dare say such things?

But is that very different from Dr. V's purpose: *"Eliminate Needless Blindness among the Poor"*?

---

[105] https://www.boringcompany.com/faq/

Or is this just the proof that this man dares to think big? And that he is much more Future-oriented than others?

Elon Musk operates under different constraints. Thus, in different spaces!

The Visions he formulates broaden the Innovation space.

They are indeed "Epic Goals" [106], opening possible paths into the Future.

Of course, he has the Money needed!

He sold ZIP 2, his first company, to Compaq for 307 million dollars in cash and 34 million in stock options in February 1999. He received 77 percent of the sale i.e. 22 million for the sale.

He also co-founded PayPal in 2001. It was acquired by eBay for 1.5 billion dollars in stock of which he received 165 million.

Yes, as it was done recently again, some people look at what he does with the Wall Street lenses and argue that his results are not always as promising as they could be.

But, after one analyst asked him what percentage of Tesla 3 reservation holders had started to configure options for their cars (an indicator of how much profit Tesla would be able to bring from the vehicles), and another analyst asked about a capital requirement before being cut off, Elon musk said:

"These questions are so dry. They're killing me,"[107]

Is it really surprising?

---

[106] https://www.inc.com/tanner-christensen/how-people-like-elon-musk-achieve-epic-innovation.html

[107] https://www.reuters.com/article/us-tesla-results/the-price-of-cutting-off-analysts-for-tesla-its-2-billion-idUSKBN1I32UC

We can also observe that Elon Musk has a certain faith in his own goals.

After all, he could enjoy a quiet life with his wife, his five children, a dog or two, a car or two (or three) and a large house (or two) anywhere.

But he doesn't stop.

He has decided to disrupt the most difficult-to-master industries in the world and he invests his own money into very risky ventures.

Can we say that those goals represent Transformative Visions?

Are we moved by them?

Do they carry a deep sense of Purpose for Humanity?

Do they enhance the Dignity of human Life?

> Some people may feel complete estranged to those goals. Maybe as some were estranged to Martin Luther king's Dream of a Fair Society? Maybe like some of us don't really feel in agreement with the "Transhumanism" dream of Immortality?
>
> The fact is that, if Elon musk succeeds in making his Visions come true, he will shape tomorrow's realities. As he is already doing it in certain fields.

At the end of a long interview, a journalist said:

> *"Thank you for dreaming so big and so precise"*.

Indeed, what is remarkable is that Elon Musk not only sees big, but also sees how!

His objectives are not just bold statements. They are accompanied by bold and in-depth investigations of how to do things. Then followed by action.

As a Wired Magazine article says:

> "When a man tells you about the time, he planned to put a vegetable garden on Mars, you worry about his mental state. But if that same man has since launched multiple rockets that are actually capable of reaching Mars—sending them into orbit, Bond-style, from a tiny island in the Pacific—you need to find another diagnosis. That's the thing about Extreme Entrepreneurialism: there's a fine line between Madness and Genius, and you need a little bit of both to really change the World." [108]

3. Anticipative Experimentation: Exploring How

Making things happen requires a vast array of skills and of strategic and creative approaches.

Failure is also possible.

Elon Musk certainly makes good use of his solid Education. (At Age twenty-four, he received a degree in Physics from the University of Pennsylvania and the same year, a degree in Economics from the Wharton School of Business.)

But Transformative Visions require Transformative Actions and Elon Musk invents his path forward.

What we can observe is the way he deep dives into "the obstacles" to make things happen, he develops very creative solutions with his teams, thinks systems and connects things in ecosystems.

First, he mobilises his Creative Intention and Energy to **disrupt** things. Not to improve them.

---

[108] https://www.wired.com/2012/10/ff-elon-musk-qa/all/

Then he dares to reinvent.

> "He is reinventing the car with Tesla, which is building all-electric vehicles in a Detroit-scale factory. ("Wired" profiled this venture in issue 18.10.) He is transforming Energy with SolarCity, a start-up that leases solar-power systems to homeowners.
>
> And he is leading the private space race with SpaceX, which is poised to replace the space shuttle and usher us into an interplanetary age. Since Musk founded the company in 2002, it has developed a series of next-generation rockets that can deliver payloads to space for a fraction of the price of legacy rockets. In 2010 SpaceX became the first private company to launch a spacecraft into orbit and bring it back; in 2012 it sent a craft to berth successfully with the International Space Station." [109]

Elon musk is also described as a man who turns complex problems into simple solutions.

> "I tend to approach things from a Physics framework," Musk said in a "Wired" Interview. Physics teaches you to reason from first principles rather than by analogy.
>
> So, I said, okay, let's look at the first principles. What is a rocket made of? Aerospace-grade aluminium alloys, plus some titanium, copper, and carbon fiber.
>
> Then I asked, what is the value of those materials on the Commodity market?

---

[109] ibid

> *It turned out that the materials cost of a rocket was around two percent of the typical price."*
>
> *Of course, there was the issue of labor and knowing how to put the pieces together. But Musk didn't let those complications stop him times, while still making a profit.*
>
> *Musk used his "First Principles Thinking" about how to break down building a rocket into the fundamental parts - the pieces he knew were absolute truths - and then looked at how he could build it more effectively from there.* [110]

In fact, Elon Musk thinks very creatively.

We define Creativity as the capacity to create Value within well identified Constraints.

In any fields he approaches, Musk excels at redefining not only the type of Value he wants to create – which is significant – but also at refining the constraints he wants to operate within (such as price, speed, etc.).

As an example, about the hyperloop tunnel, you can read

> *Why hasn't this been done before?*
>
> *Currently, tunnels are really expensive to dig, with some projects costing as much as $1 billion per mile.*

So, no discussion...just constraints.

> *To make a tunnel network feasible, tunnelling costs must be reduced by a factor of more than ten.*

---

[110] https://www.inc.com/jory-mackay/how-elon-musk-used-this-simple-mental-strategy-to-build-2-billion-dollar-businesses.html

THE ART OF SHAPERSHIP

And then, obviously, the search for a creative solution

How can we reduce the cost of tunnelling?

First, reduce the tunnel diameter. The current standard for a one-lane tunnel is approximately twenty-eight feet. By placing vehicles on a stabilized electric skate, the diameter can be reduced to less than fourteen feet. Reducing the diameter in half reduces tunnelling costs by three-four times.

Second, increase the speed of the Tunnel Boring Machine (TBM). TBMs are super slow. A snail is effectively fourteen times faster than a soft-soil TBM. Our goal is to defeat the <u>snail</u> **in a race.** [111]

It is true that his goals are related to the **eco-system** and that his solutions are based on **connecting** elements and creating synergies.

For instance, in 2012, Musk announced that SolarCity and Tesla Motors were collaborating to use electric vehicle batteries to smooth the impact of rooftop solar Energy on the power grid, with the program going live in 2013.

After an earlier envisioning of the Hyperloop, Musk assigned a dozen engineers from Tesla Motors and Space X who worked together for nine months, establishing the conceptual foundations and creating the designs for the new transportation system.

As written in an article entitled "How Elon Musk Comes Up with Epic Ideas? A Simple Strategy, actually":

"If you want to achieve goals on the same level as Elon Musk, Thomas Edison, Marie Curie,

---

[111] see the website for details https://goo.gl/JcLXgQ

> *Steve Jobs, or IDEO CEO Tim Brown, pursue many varying interests at the same time. Pursuing a number of diverse interests is an effective way to gain insights, stumble on atypical solutions to problems, and stay creative."*[112]

Is that the way an entrepreneur would do?

Probably "Yes".

Is that the way a Shaper would do?

> The idea is that what makes Elon Musk more than a "South African-born American Business magnate, investor and engineer" is that he apparently connects the three elements that make the DNA of Shapership™:
>
> 1) Creative Resistance
>
> 2) Transformative Vision
>
> 3) Anticipative Experimentation
>
> We were tempted to call him a "Shaper of innovative Life Sustaining Solutions".
>
> But we intuitively feel that Elon Musk does not really fit with the concept of Shapers.

Why not?

Shapers radically challenge the status quo, he does.

Shapers operate from the Future, he does.

Shapers open new paths to the Future, he does, with "epic goals".

> But it seems to us that Elon Musk differs from the Shapers on two main aspects:

---

[112] https://www.inc.com/tanner-christensen/how-people-like-elon-musk-achieve-epic-innovation.html

- What makes Shapers very specific is their Humanity, their posture which aim at restoring or enhancing the Dignity of Human beings and the Meaning of Human Life

- Shapers don't usually sense and seize opportunities to make things "better or faster" within the same paradigm: Shapers open transformative paths to the Future which redefine Respect, Hope, Justice, Success, in a transformative way which escapes the dominant system worldviews and logic, especially those of neo-liberal capitalism. They put themselves at the service of a cause and drive pioneering Wealth-creation in an "alternative" paradigm, based on radically different values and worldviews.

Chapter 8

Shapership™ as a practice

Potentially, anyone with a strong Vision for improving Society and/or their Community can become a Shaper

What is irrelevant is name, origin, colour, social background, Education or position.

What is essential is a state of Consciousness and of Coherence.

Shapership™ might be an inspiration to anyone to become a Shaper of the Future or to add certain dimensions of Shapership™ to their current existence.

In fact, Shapership™ is a way to make a creative deconstruction and reconstruction of our beliefs about the world and our place in it.

It is a "lens" to make more conscious decisions on how we want to be, to become, to participate to the transformation of "the world" and face the issues of our time.

We all have the same desire to make sense of our lives, each of us in his/her own way. Almost all of us have - in the back or in the front of our Minds, at different "periods of our

Life— some of the most important questions that we can possibly ask in this time of Global Shift:

- What kind of world do we want to live in?
- Do I have a role in helping to create that world?
- What is my Purpose in this Life?
- What contribution do I want to make?

In this book, we have chosen to tell the story of some "famous" Shapers.

Some readers have told us they liked those stories but – and remember that everything that comes before the "but" is bullshit – that they could not identify with those examples. Meaning they "felt" too small or too powerless, compared to those "heroes"!

Comparison is an effective way to find "excuses", but it does not necessarily lead to Inspiration.

The idea is that "Thinking Big and Radical" about "the" world we want to shape needs to be done within the appropriate scope, i.e. the one we chose: "our" world.

Actually, the Shapership™ Attitude is adopted by people and "communities of work" - Citizens, Students, Bakers, Teachers, Managers, Leaders, Entrepreneurs, Networks, Practitioners of Health, Communities of farmers, and many others.

It is their Life they want to change. They want to escape from one which limits their sense of possibility to a preferred story which gives them space to be, to grow and make sense of their Life.

They want to shape a viable and desirable Future at the "local level": within their family, their communities, their organizations, their "territories" or their field of practice.

They want to imagine what is possible, not only for their lives but for their relations, their "territories", sometimes their nation, even the whole Humanity.

And since we all live within larger contexts, changing one's Life is a political act: it demands to challenge the taken for granted discourse and cultural beliefs (about death, power, health, education, control, success, etc.) that shape the meaning of our Life, at a given time and in a specific context.

So, anyone who deeply aspire to create a new story of the Future based on different worldviews, needs to be ready to cross the threshold from the tamed territories of the "Reasonable" to the untamed territories of a "new Imaginary".

That aspiration leads some people to put their Imagination, Courage, Soul, Wisdom, Creativity and Passion at work to shape the Future.

This is the Shapership™ Attitude that anyone can adopt.

Everyday.

We feel that no one is born a Shaper but that anyone can become one!

This entire book is the illustration of ways through which Shapers manifest themselves and operate.

There are no "recipes" or "toolbox" required to "develop" that "State of Being" and this "Craft".

But there are certainly keys and practices which help to "activate" and adopt the Shapership™ Attitude.

Shapership's DNA is one the keys that can trigger that capacity within ourselves.

Another practice is to align oneself in Conscience and Coherence with the three shifts.

THE ART OF SHAPERSHIP

Here are series of additional elements to support the applications as sources of pragmatic inspiration and reflective surfaces.

"Mapping the Maps"

Remember that "the Art of Shaping the Future" is about the Power and the Freedom to reconsider the stories we tell ourselves to change our own Reality.

That is possible thanks to a series of Shifts in Thinking and Perspectives.

At its core, the Shapership™ Attitude suggests to "make the Future the cause of the Present". It demands to entertain the best we can Future Consciousness – the Awareness of the Future in the "Now" - and to cultivate deliberately the sense of Hope and Purpose in what we are doing.

These expanded awareness and worldviews might really help us - at an individual level, as well as the collective level of families, teams, communities, organizations, societies and nations - to make wiser decisions towards shaping action "Now Here".

In a period, which carries within itself as many dangers as genuine opportunities, we are all facing a polarisation in our everyday Life

- either we are prisoners of **Regression forces** -Fear, Egos, Lack of Imagination, Despair, Fatalisation and a craving for Certitude - which creates the risk of our going back to repeating the same old solutions, short-term decisions, Competition, Authorities, Polarisations and Exclusions

- or we are **guided by Opening Forces** we carry within ourselves such as Courage, Hope, Creative

Energy, Imagination, which may lead us to shape a different and viable Future [113]

The key rests in the way we look at the world, in other words, in our capacity to "Map our Mental Maps" and the landscapes they let us see.

"Mapping the maps" means:

- Becoming aware of the "stories" we create and mapping their effects on our lives, in every domain
- Reconsidering, challenging and escaping those we don't want
- Opening our Future awareness, unlocking our Imagination and Heart to let alternative and preferred stories emerge
- Weaving meaningful and committed relationship with the Future we desire for ourselves and our Society
- Making conscious and wise choices based on freer and expanded perspectives.

Shifting our Perspectives means consciously trying new points of views to transform the way we see the world and our place in it.

The "Me Map" shows this possibility to consciously navigate our own landscape, moving in various directions

- Looking backward: Re-Thinking and Re-perceiving the Past
- Looking forward: Re-Imagining the Future
- Moving up: Re-opening the Space.

---

[113] *You may want to look back at the insert 4 for more details about the steps towards freedom and the obstacles to overcome*

THE ART OF SHAPERSHIP

From looking inward - in an EGO centric perspective - to looking upward: taking the Altitude Attitude, being able to step back, seeing the Big Picture and Thinking big, seeing and listening in ways that open new doors to possibilities, feeling with all our senses

- Moving "North East": Re-storying the Future with a meaningful and Transformative Vision - a "Counter Story", No Where - which opens a new lens, full of Hope and desires

- Moving Back from the Future: Re-considering and Re-Storying the Present: the priorities and decisions we make Now Here.

Insert 10: The "Me Map"

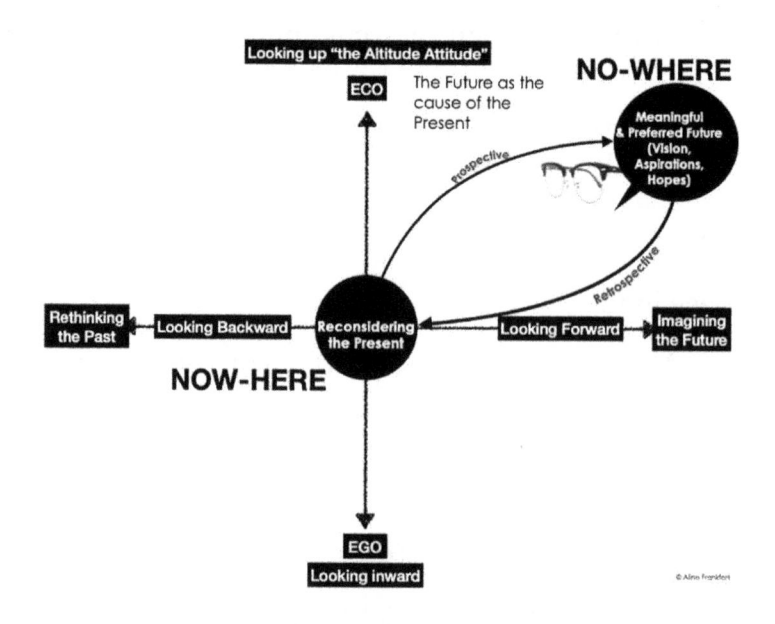

Thinking about the way we Think

The Art of Shaping the Future demands to unfold the deep skills of Wisdom, Creativity and Reflection. They enhance our Freedom to live in a world, outside "Plato's Cave", unchained from the "prison" of our representations.

But to unchain ourselves, we need to recognize that we are chained; we need to see that what is projected on the screen of our Mind are just ideas, representations, stories that "write" our Life.

We need to attend our own "Theatre of the Mind". And decide whether we want to attend the same performance all our lives. Or chose a preferred one.

And this is not necessarily painful. It might even be a lot of fun.

As Einstein said: *"There are only two ways to live one's life. One as if nothing is a miracle. The other as if everything is a miracle."*

It is time for us to be able to transform what we think and how we think about what we think.

We need to take the Altitude Attitude "in our mind".

At least, we need to be able to reflect on how we think, i.e. to think about the way we think.

This requires making our "invisible" maps visible, i.e., to recognize, reassess and question the everyday taken for granted structure of assumptions, beliefs, so called "Truths" and points of views that constitute our identity and shape the meaning of our lives.

By making them visible, we can make our familiar routines and Thinking habits strange to us. We can discover how they sometimes alienate us by distorting our understanding and our sense of possibility.

We can look at how we are shaped by these stories and how we keep them alive.

That also leads us to become fully aware of the way we contribute to preserve the Past, maintain the Status quo or Shape the New.

To find inner Rightness, we also have to challenge those disembodied ways of speaking up that hide biases, prejudices, and "correct" answers to incorrectly asked questions that we have never really thought about freely.

We have to understand the relationship between the quality of our Thinking and the quality of our Future.

Thinking is resisting. It is contradicting the "stuck" experience that leads to lack of Agency, repetitive dialogues and solutions. It brings forward a new sense of Awareness and Infinite Possibilities, so that we can ignite Imagination, Hope, Freedom, Pride and Dignity.

The "Creative Thinking" imperative

That would deserve an entire book but here are just a few sentences.

To design innovative ways forward and shape our Future for the best, it is vital to move away from just recognising "known" situations and repeat standard answers.

Today's challenges invite us to tap on all the Creativity and Knowledge at our disposal. They require a Creative – even "Revolutionary", not incremental – Thinking to invent viable solutions for the "wicked" problems now facing our lives.

All of us need to become "Shapers of Future Context", to explore the Future with Imagination.

We need to become Thoughtful and Mindful people who have the courage, the flexibility and the capacity to see things differently and to creatively reinvent our approaches instead of just "rearranging" the furniture in the same room.

Instead of being under the pressure to conform, looking for the one right formula or the tested Truth", we need to cultivate Creative Thinking as a skill.

That will allow us to escape all the "prisons" of our mind - such as the prisons of Repetition, Rigidity, Conventional Wisdom, "incremental Thinking" - and to put our Imagination at work with Audacity to open up radically new ways forward versus solving or fixing the problem.

That will allow us to "make the seemingly impossible possible".

At a time when everyone is rushing headlong into action and into the so-called "Concrete Realism", we need to relearn the value of reflection and master Conceptual Thinking which is in fact the essence of Creativity. This is needed to connect Vision and Action and navigate this fuzzy and ambiguous world with pleasure.

Rehearsing the Future

Here is how to Think "radical" (back to the essence /roots) and apply the "Altitude Attitude" in our daily private and professional Life, alone and in groups.

Look at the DNA of Shapership™ – the big No, the big Yes and Creative Experimentation – as a practice which allows a "Rehearsal of the Future"

Rehearsing our Future is possible.

It is one of the most efficient ways to escape the "repetition" of the S.O.S (Same Old Solutions) and to give voice to our aspirations.

THE ART OF SHAPERSHIP

This is a way to individually and/or collectively rewrite the relationship we have with our "current" situation, invent an alternative story in line with our Hopes, Aspirations, Values and Dreams. And then, to get from where we are to where we want to go.

In other words, this is an invitation to shift from

- an experience of "being stuck": a "current" and Known situation which is non-Fit for the Future, which limits our sense of possibility - what we think and how we think

- to an experience of being "Unstuck": a counter and as yet "unknown" Future we imagine, which is at the same time viable and desirable

At this point, what is required is to put the DNA of Shapership™ into Practice

Insert 11: The DNA of Shapership™ in Practice

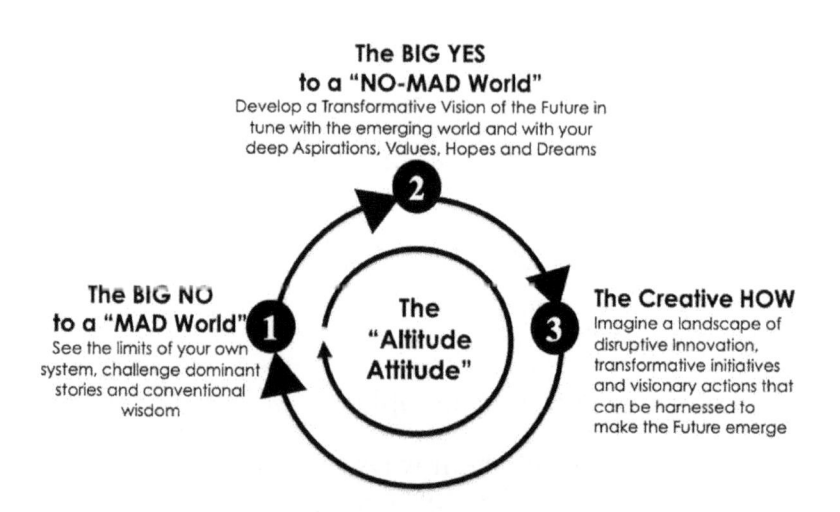

The BIG YES to a "NO-MAD World"
Develop a Transformative Vision of the Future in tune with the emerging world and with your deep Aspirations, Values, Hopes and Dreams

The BIG NO to a "MAD World"
See the limits of your own system, challenge dominant stories and conventional wisdom

The "Altitude Attitude"

The Creative HOW
Imagine a landscape of disruptive Innovation, transformative initiatives and visionary actions that can be harnessed to make the Future emerge

We can imagine applying this to one of our major question or challenge – a way to make bread, the strategies we adopt, the way we approach health - and move step by step, although it might be an iterative movement:

1. Creative Resistance: The Big "NO" to a "MAD World"

This is about "deconstructing" our world: challenging the way it is and our "routines" that maintain it

1) Seeing "the normal way things are" (in your defined scope) with fresh eyes and mapping the Landscape of current concerns: looking at the evidences, signs, trends which show that the current approaches (system, structures, strategies, actors, worldviews) are not viable for the Future: they are no longer Fit for Purpose

2) Making the invisible Visible: identifying the taken for granted beliefs, ideas and assumptions that might keep us stuck.

3) Mapping the consequences and sequels: how are these ideas influencing us? What are their effects and influence on our life, our relations, our customers, our employees, our partnerships, our strategies?

4) Refreshing our mental maps: questioning and deconstructing the obvious, escaping the "prison" of representations

5) Taking a stand in line with our preferences. activate Courage, Creative Resistance, even Anger, Imagination and Desire. See where we want to say a big No.

2. Transformative Vision: The Big "YES" to a "NO-MAD World"

This is about "Reconstructing" our Future world: seeing the Unknown Future as a potential of infinite possibilities, offering opportunities for alternative and preferred stories of our Future, including who we are, who we have been, who we would prefer to be and might decide to become.

We are called to activate the Opening forces: Hope, imagination, Dignity, Poetry and Freedom

1) Connecting to our "implicit" Big Yes: with an open "Soul Compass", listening to all our voices, our Hopes, our Values, Dreams and Aspirations for a preferred Future. Feeling what wants to die and what wants to emerge

2) Re-imagining and making the Unseen visible: mapping our Future possibilities, expanding our perspectives and giving birth to a vision of a radically different Future, fully supported and supporting those Values and Hopes

3) Remembering and connecting to the Future which is already "Now" but unseen. Finding "Pockets of the Future in the Present": unique initiatives, actions, events - from our life or other people's life, anywhere in the world, in the Past or right now - which are "traces" of the Counter Story and are fully in line with our Vision

4) Reconnecting to our own knowledges, gifts, faith, wisdom, unique capacities and actions

5) Re-storing: "imaging" a rich, Meaning-Making Counter Story of our Future, to which we say a Big Yes and which includes the impact we want to have in this world

6) Mapping the consequences: see how this new story might shape our Lives

3. Anticipative Experimentation: The Creative "HOW"

This is the time and space in which the Metamorphosis of the Caterpillar into a Butterfly takes place.

The "Creative How" is about mapping the Landscape of Action and Innovation: making the bold "transition" path towards our Vision Visible and actionable, seeing at the same time

- the actions that need to be taken today to address our issues and concerns
- the far-sighted and transformative actions to get to our preferred Future.

It is also creating a pertinent collaboration and "clustering" strategy among the "imaginal cells": building a "community of Purpose", rallying a formidable ecosystem of actors as co-innovators and co-adaptors, respecting their Agency, Mutuality and Dignity while serving a common Vision.

This Transition "space" is also the place to disrupt the system with a Purpose, *"building a new model that makes the existing model obsolete"*.

This might inspire Entrepreneurs who pursue promising and innovative projects. They indeed can become Shapers if they add a real "Transformative Vision" to what they do and manage their "innovations" to trigger the shift towards a new paradigm, rather than to be captured by people who just want to do "more of the same, better".

THE ART OF SHAPERSHIP

Here are a few examples the DNA of Shapership™ in practice

For instance, a teacher can express a big NO to Mediocrity, say a big YES to helping students accomplish their full potential and invent a creative teaching method to help them succeed.

This is Ben Zander, the Boston Symphony Orchestra's conductor! He teaches students ranging from early age to their teens. And he is fed up with the tradition "grade" system which encourages doubt, competition, comparison and limitations. He believes in "infinite possibilities".

At the beginning of their first class, he tells them they already are getting an A for their class! At one condition: they must write him a letter three months later, dated a year from now, telling him what and how they did to get that A!

Result: the Future is the cause of the Present! From that day on, he only has A students in his class - not musicians asking themselves if they are

going to deserve an A later – but Musicians who already "are" A students!

A Baker can say NO to bad bread and to waste, totally commit to manufacture a delicious product and invent new approaches to his trade.

There is a baker who decided to stop a "blind" mass production" a part of which he threw away every day. He decided to work two days a week and to manufacture bread of outstanding quality – i.e. the freshness of which "lasts" longer – for the Community around him.

He spends the rest of the time taking care of his vegetable garden and studying Astronomy! Clients can come buy their bread whenever they want, even if he is not there! They just leave the money on the counter in total confidence.

That baker says he has never been as happy in his entire Life and his financial situation has never been as good!

One day, an old farmer realized that because of his old-fashioned production methods - GMOs, pesticides, etc. - he had ruined his soil so badly that he could not even leave his farm to his children.

He said a big No.

He said a big yes to "Regenerative Agriculture".

And he is building an ecosystem of farmers ready to learn and apply together these new practices that restore dignity to their profession, complementing each other, in a collective strategy of regeneration of the territory, those who live there and the future generations.

The three necessary shifts to give life to Shapership™

There are internal shifts and alignments that anyone can operate:

- a shift in Intentions: moving from the Desire to preserve the Past to the Desire to shape the Future and to make a difference
- a shift in Emotions: moving from the Fear and Despair to Hope, Desire and Hope
- a shift in Thinking; moving from Linear and Analytical Thinking, centred on Ego, to Complex and Creative Thinking, organized on real Eco-system issues

Insert 11: the three Shifts needed to embody Shapership™

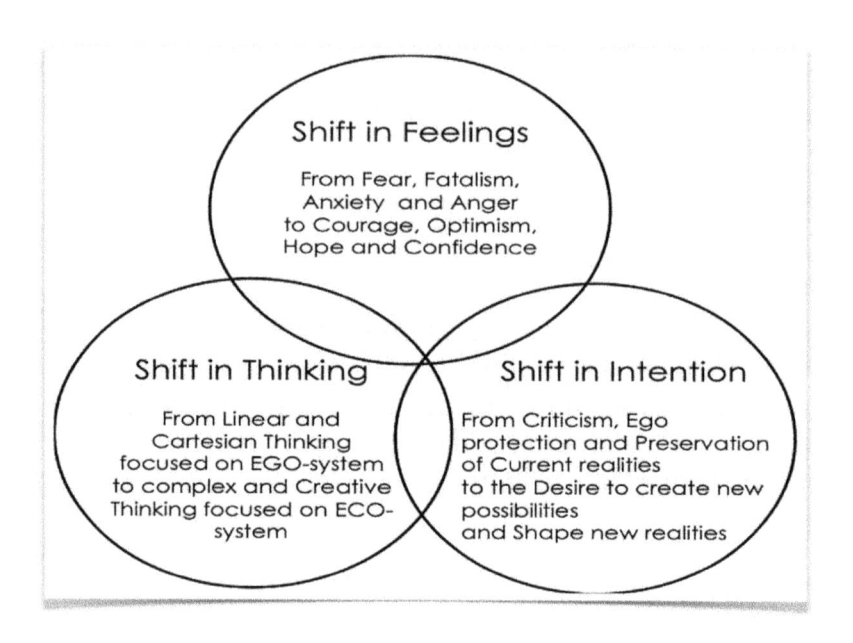

Shift in Feelings
From Fear, Fatalism, Anxiety and Anger to Courage, Optimism, Hope and Confidence

Shift in Thinking
From Linear and Cartesian Thinking focused on EGO-system to complex and Creative Thinking focused on ECO-system

Shift in Intention
From Criticism, Ego protection and Preservation of Current realities to the Desire to create new possibilities and Shape new realities

What will not lead to Shapership™?
1. The intention to preserve the Status Quo, Critical Thinking and defeatism, destruction, the will to protect one's Ego or at least one's conception of it

What may lead to Shapership™?
1. Start from an intention to build the Future, to create life-generating solutions, to have a constructive impact and to serve real needs, to focalize on outcomes, start with the end result in mind, be it eliminate needless Blindness like Dr. V did, or create an affordable test for pancreatic cancer like Jack Andraka did or stimulate Imagination in relation with the Unconscious as an artist friend of ours puts it!

2. Emotions such as Fear either to lose or not have enough, to miss, to lack knowledge, not to be loved which usually lead to confusion, paralysis and dependence

2. Operate with an open Heart, from emotions which stimulate Imagination and Creativity. Feel at our deepest level our desires and aspirations – we could even talk about our soul and align ourselves with that reality which inspires Courage, Optimism, Hope and Confidence. When we are in that "Rightness" state, we never let a shadow of a doubt darken our days

3. Rational Thinking disconnected from emotions, which lead to premeditation, calculations, repetition and rarely to Inspiration

3. Open our Mind to allow a broad and inspired reflexion, able to take our own representations and beliefs, to challenge our own hypothesis, to play with concepts and imagine new possibilities.

These three shifts make it possible to be inspired before doing! And to bring another type of Inspiration in our actions.

What actually counts is to align, in conscience and coherence, the three dimensions of one's being. This shift is going to completely re-orient – i.e. give meaning and a direction – to Life and the choices each person will make.

And the shift can be understood and even made rapidly in certain cases.

For example, a man in his late thirties comes to see us. He is developing a nice career in the United-States, makes a comfortable living, works a lot, never had any kind of "accident" except that his current boss wants to fire him! And he knows it!

Why? Cost reductions!

He comes to see us to prepare his negotiation.

His goal is to obtain a maximum of compensation.

Why? To guarantee his security!

He is afraid of an imaginary catastrophe and he wants to have enough money to go on living!

To do what?

To find another job, continue to build a career and ensure his security.

As long as he remains in this irrational state of Fear, the conversation revolves around his Ego needs. The state of Fear is irrational because, in fact, his security is not threatened at all!

But nothing else seems to exist, no other need seems to be taken into account is his potential choices.

Our conversation totally shifts when we present him with the perspectives Shapership™ can offer!

In the bottom of his heart, what actually motivates this man are a Big No and a Big Yes.

The Dream Project he carries in his heart is based on his personal revolt against the fact that Belgium's industrial context is unravelling, especially in fields most dear to him like Chocolate and biscuits, following the sale of "jewels" to foreign financial groups.

In the bottom of his heart, he has a big dream: to rebuild a prosperous ecosystem in his preferential fields, based on local know-hows, competences and talents which yearn to express themselves, shine and spread.

This is a Shaper's Transformative Vision.

His "Soul Compass" knows how to guide him from there. Let his Life be driven by his Desires, his Values, his Aspiration and no longer his fears (real or imaginary).

The rest of the story is obvious: he wants to negotiate his departure to dedicate himself to this "desired Future".

The negotiation took place in a serene atmosphere rather than looking for another job to ensure his security. The man activated his neurons and his networks to rally an ecosystem of actors who are going to carry the dream forward with him.

We did not turn this man into a Shaper! The "word" Shapership™ opened a window in his mind.

The articulation of the Shapership's DNA immediately made sense to him and allowed him to express himself as a Shaper!

Another example. Recently, in a train, a young entrepreneur tells us about his Life. He manages a somewhat ailing company.

He is imprisoned in Industrialization and selling one product for over ten years.

His dream is to recreate in his Region (also ailing) an ecosystem of actors. He has lost sight of that project for a long time. He has ceased hoping. He has abandoned the idea of imagining another Future for him and for his Region

Here again, when we mention the DNA of Shapership™, the man suddenly wakes up. He adopts the "Altitude Attitude" and begins to describe the diversification he wishes to carry on, to challenge his "unique" product (the one and only he has) which represents his core Business. In other words, his mental "jail" as it were! He gets off the train with stars in his eyes and clear intentions.

Behind any Fear, a Desire

"Emotions" are "what puts us in motion".

Each one of us can start moving for a series of reasons! But one of the most fundamental elements is to feel if our choices and our actions are driven by our Fears – real or perceived – or by our Desires!

To us, the opposite of Fear is Desire.

Fear tends to maintain us in an "Ego-centric" perspective, locked in the Past.

Desires and Hopes tend to uplift our perspectives, to place ourselves at the service of Life, in a movement towards the Future.

But the thing is that behind any Fear, there is often a Desire.

The Fear of not being loved has a mirror in a desire to be unconditionally loved.

The fear of being "imprisoned" implicitly talks about the Hopes and Desire for Freedom.

Look at the insert and the mirroring effect.

Insert 12

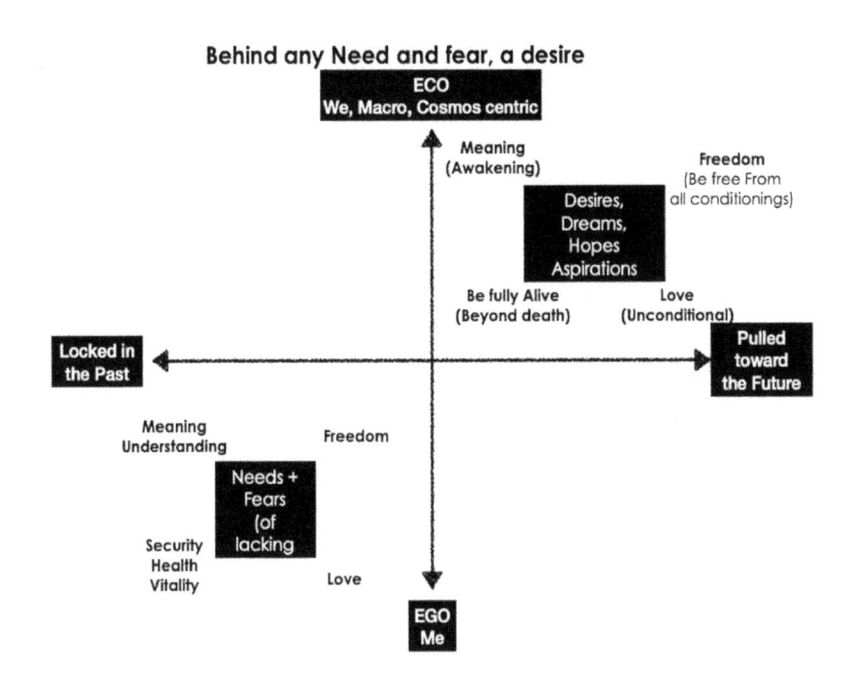

Behind any Need and fear, a desire

```
                    ECO
            We, Macro, Cosmos centric
                     ▲
              Meaning
             (Awakening)              Freedom
                          Desires,   (Be free From
                          Dreams,    all conditionings)
                          Hopes
                          Aspirations
              Be fully Alive      Love
              (Beyond death)     (Unconditional)
  Locked in                              Pulled
  the Past  ◄─────────────────────────► toward
                                        the Future
        Meaning       Freedom
        Understanding
                    Needs +
                     Fears
                     (of
         Security    lacking)
         Health
         Vitality    Love
                      ▼
                    EGO
                     Me
```

Four fundamental fears linked with deficits and lacks (real or perceived)

- Lack of Vitality (disease, depression, fatigue, burn out)
- Lack of Meaning (absurdity, Bore out, etc.)
- Lack of Freedom (Dominance, imprisonment of all sorts, dogmatism, censorship, lack of autonomy)
- Lack of Love (empathy, sympathy, kindness, warmth, respect)

Four fundamental desires mirroring those fears

- Desire for Life
- Desire for Meaning
- Desire for Freedom
- Desire for Love

In real Life, these aspects coexist but it is our capacity to balance them that will lead us towards Shapership™: we need to take our Fears into consideration and, without fighting "against" them nor being driven by them, build an alternative "meaning-making" story of our Life that includes our Hopes and Desires.

Saying a big Yes will allow us to overcome Fears and to shape an alternative Future named "Desire".

As an example, here is a team about to launch a revolutionary medical invention but locked in a similar type of tension between Fear and Desire.

Part of the young researchers, coming from a university, were struck by panic when they realized that the invention would only be viable if it was carried by a new structure, i.e., a start-up.

At that very moment, all their energy immediately focused on one question: "Am I going to keep my job?"

So, here are a number of people who panic about their short-term Future, whereas they are on the verge of developing an invention that may revolutionize a medical treatment applicable to millions of people!

They adopt the caterpillar attitude: they fight for the preservation of the Status Quo. Although they are perfectly aware that their current medical treatment is showing signs of obsolescence and is not viable for the Future.

They are ready to commit suicide.

In the same Group, other people are like "imaginal cells": they see the Future in the Present. They understand that what they are doing is a prototype of the Future and they adopt Butterfly Thinking.

The whole group enters into a dialogue about the Future, shifting from rigid Mindsets to flexible perspectives, listening deeply to all the voices.

Is it the fear of losing or the desire to make a difference that is going to drive them?

They start to shift perspectives. They say a Big No to leading the wrong fights.

They say a Big Yes and they all commit to live the metamorphosis and give birth to an extraordinary new healing approach!

Potentially, they were Shapers. They consciously decided to become Shapers.

We all know people who crossed the threshold and moved from a quite but unsatisfactory Life to a new Life that was more meaningful for them. They make a choice to serve Life.

Rather than being restricted by our Fears, which are a "representation", our "Soul Compass" can help us reach the inner rightness and make decisions with our Mind, our Heart, and our Will wide open, in the direction of Life.

Shapership™ can provide us with a lens and an inspiration to make more conscious decisions on who we want to be.

Chapter 9

What can Shapership™ bring to organizations and Businesses?

Everything which has been said in the previous Chapters is applicable by "Communities of work", Networks, Companies, and organizations of all sorts, because organizations are made by People, with people – although not always for People.

A "business" that works is a "business" you believe in. The same for an institution.

It is a belief system, a story that makes sense. Or not.

Think of Apple for example, and Steve Job's high Masses.

There is a "spirit" that adds an intangible Value to a company, beyond what it does.

The Philosopher Alain Etchegoyen has even written a book about it in 1994, "Do companies have a soul?" And guess what? The answer was yes. Because people put a part of their soul in everything they do. So, if they feel it is bad for their soul, they become disengaged. [114]

Since the Future people imagine is changing their experience of Reality "Now Here", all organizations need a sense of "direction": they all have to create a "Meaning-making" story of their Future in a turbulent world. This is even more true since the Covid-19 pandemic which, for a number of industries, has in a way, abruptly kidnapped their Future.

But Shapership™ is not for everyone. Because Shapership™ is nor a toolbox, nor a fashion or the next thing that can be kidnapped to make as if things make sense.

The sense of Integrity built in the Shapership™ Attitude is this: it supports the fabric of Life.

Let's come back one moment to the idea that what makes Life meaningful is that it has a Future. As we said earlier,

> "And what makes that Life has a future? It is that, at some point, there's something great and awesome that pulls everything else together: Nobility, Dignity, Beauty, Greatness, Elevation: that is the Future."

Building a Future on those aspects is what makes Life exciting, what we are ready to give a part of our soul for.

That is also what can make a company or an organisation exciting.

Well, at this point in time, some companies don't have a Future.

---

[114] For example, people who worked for a large mineral water company say that, considering water as a natural resource that belongs to everyone, they lived like thieves because their company only tapped water from the ground, then bottled it with a label and sold it at a high price. Their company was making money but not contributing to the fabric of Life and they completely disengaged.

Some because they are soulless machines, too inwardly focused on the old story of "Scarcity", Profit and Value capture; some because they are just able to provide people with "bullshit jobs" but unable to provide them with the sense of Hope, Meaning and Purpose in what they do. Others because they have not kept up to speed with a changing world and they are now fighting for the survival of the caterpillar, ready to kill the "imaginal cells" or to "capture them" in order to ensure the preservation of their own "voracious" system.

At this specific moment where MAD Land is showing how "unfit for the Future" it is, even within a world colonized by "Capitalism Realism", "having a corporate job" and the perspective of "making a carrier" is no longer enough to provide a meaning to Life.

> *"Life in industrial modernity might have been alienating and boring, a life for specialists without minds, pleasure seekers without heart, as Weber wrote in the concluding pages on his essay on the protestant Ethic. But at least, people's existential security was in some sense shielded. You could toil on your own corporate job faithful that, somehow, in the grand scheme of things, what you did made a difference and contributed to a greater cause.*
>
> *When these grand narratives have evaporated, "the Bullshit" nature of many corporate jobs reveals itself. Indeed, David Graber, who coined the terms, suggests that about 40 percent of workers in middle management jobs like PR, human resources, brand managers or financial consultants "feel their jobs are pointless". Many people now escape such careers if they can, sensing that a bulshit job will not allow them to make the*

kind of change they desire, or even to realize their own ambitions".[115]

Businesses and organizations need to change their "Spirit", "Souls" and Stories.

They are facing the need to collectively rewrite their relationships with the dominant system and worldviews of MAD Land.

Can we say that they need to take a stand: fight for the survival of the caterpillar or play their role, as imaginative cells, to contribute to the metamorphosis into the Butterfly?

It is a moment to escape the orthodox approaches, conventional Wisdom that only serve to preserve the Past, maintain the status quo or "fix the problem".

It is time to build "Transformative Visions" of viable and preferred Futures.

And then to transition from the Caterpillar into the Butterfly, in other words, to innovate.

But this absolutely needs to be clear: we need to revisit what we call Innovation in these times of craziness. Because Innovation is such a buzzword that the main danger today is to be stuck into lip service approaches and to fail asking the question: why should we innovate?

You may feel that this question is totally irrelevant because, implicitly, there is a shared belief that Innovation will of course generate a "new" that will be better than what currently exists.

But what is the purpose of Innovation? What does it serve?

Is it meant to ensure the survival of our failing neoliberal system which, in the name of the Sacro-saint myth of Growth,

---

[115] Changemakers, the industrious Future of the Digital Economy, Adam Ardvinsson, Polity Edition, page 4

has generated unparalleled levels of environmental, social and economic damages?

Is it designed to bring so-called disruptive answers which exploit the opportunities of the changing world by proposing solutions which are indeed more "*efficient*" but often articulated around the same logic?

Or is genuine Innovation meant to intentionally shift a system towards a desirable and viable Future, thanks to visionary and transformative approaches which escape the dominant system worldviews and logic?

If yes, Innovation is the "Creative Experimentation" (The Creative How) serving a Transformative Vision (the Big Yes): Innovation is the bold path to shape the Future we desire.

As it is brilliantly demonstrated by the "Three Horizons Framework" developed by Bill Sharpe, American economist [116], without these more inspiring perspectives, we remain locked in the existing paradigm and the dominant stories of Scarcity, Separation, Competition, Infinite Growth, which we know is unsustainable in the long-term.

As a consequence, most of the time, what is called "Innovation" is mainly captured to correct and maintain the current ailing system in place, or to "disrupt" it, using approaches which may be more efficient, but which do not fundamentally challenge Values, Power Games and Goals that are becoming more and more unsustainable. We "navigate" in an ever more complex landscape using obsolete maps which dangerously lack Imagination and Pertinence.

The Art of Shaping the Future depends on our capacity to "challenge" our ways of Thinking and Seeing – our perceptions, our visions of the world, our beliefs – to open new possibilities, invent the meaning-making story and the models of a viable and hope-carrying Future.

---

[116] Three Horizons: the Patterning of Hope, Bill Sharpe, triarchy Press

Shapership™ is a practice that Organizations and Businesses can adopt.

After all, they are not abstract entities but communities of people.

Why limit "Strategic Vision" and "Innovation" to rational exercises, dominated by "Ego Needs", the desire to control, predict, win over, defeat, eliminate, kill, sell more and make profit endangering the planet?

Why not instead consider the same words with the Shapership™ "Altitude Attitude" and an open "Soul Compass? That would means connecting Heads, Hands, and Guts to dare Transformative Visions which really answers their aspirations, their "Soul needs", and are in tune with the imperatives of our times.

This Shapership™ attitude may be adopted by any "community of work" which aspires to drive pioneering Wealth-Creation in an "alternative" paradigm, based on radically different Values and worldviews that might lead Humanity to become more humane.

And you know what? "Pockets of the Future already exist today"! We see the emergence of Businesses which are moving from "EGO"-system to "ECO"-system approaches to face the major imperatives of our time.

Some organizations are shifting from "competing to sell more thermometers" – focusing inwardly on their activities or products" – to collaborating on reducing the temperature: fighting together for the right and meaningful system issues.

They demonstrate that other ways of doing are possible and desirable. They illustrate "Transformative" innovations based on totally different Visions and Values, much more in tune with the changes happening in the world and the imperatives we must face.

The case of Novamont, which we developed earlier in this book is one example. Many other exist, deeply committed to serve the Fabric of Life and to promote "Regenerative Economy".

They see themselves as imaginative cells which can leverage a metamorphosis into a NO MAD world.

As Harvard Business Review puts it in a quite radical article published in April 2017:

> **"Prosperity in a Society is the accumulation of solutions to human problems.**
>
> *By emphasizing solutions as the engine of Growth, Beinhocker and Hanauer wanted to cast capitalism as a force for Prosperity (as the system that churns out the most constant stream of superior ones). But their way of Thinking about Prosperity also offers direction for any managers who want to work harder to make the world better off: your Mission is to imagine, develop, and launch more life-improving solutions, especially the kinds of goods and services that improve ordinary people's lives.*
>
> *Businesses have a variety of social responsibilities, but the essential one—and the main reason that private enterprise is given license to operate—is to innovate.* "[117]

---

[117] Meaningful work should not be a privilege of the Elite, Harvard Business review, April 2017. https://hbr.org/2017/04/meaningful-work-should-not-be-a-privilege-of-the-elite,

For these new Businesses, the "Olympic minimum" is to be fully aligned with Value Creation on the "4 P bottom Lines":

- People   Social Well-Being
- Planet   Environmental Health
- Profit   Economy
- Purpose   Meaning

Even Forbes Magazine, which is not particularly a left-wing publication, talks about *"the quadruple promise of People, Planet, Profit, and Purpose"*. [118]

Those organisations are driven by Outcomes. They connect Purpose with Profitability.

Profit is the reward for the Value they create.

They make "purpose" their bottom line.

And they consciously chose to disrupt the System with a Purpose.

Because it makes sense.

True Leaders are not prisoners of the Dominant System

When they realise that they are in the "prison of the Mind", they do not choose to improve their incarceration - to make the prison more agreeable, to put thicker carpets and pictures on the walls. They have the courage to get out.

Recently, a company belonging to an industry seriously affected by COVID-19 came to see us.

No more customers.

---

[118] Forbes magazine, 15th December 2016, The Top Trends Shaping Business for 2017. https://www.forbes.com/sites/marymeehan/2016/12/15/the-top-trends-shaping-business-for-2017/#22ca89ac6a8a

Until then, they were in great shape; they had a bright Future ahead of them. Even if we can say that they belong to an Industry that, in itself, symbolises the MAD Land model: big polluting machines relying on intensive use of fossil fuels, a lot of useless transport from one end of the world to the other.

So, except for the blind ones, this is an Industry whose Long-Term Future is not viable, if they keep doing "business as usual".

Suddenly, here comes COVID-19 which steals that Future from them (their Future is now behind them).

Confusion reigns, Despair and Fear undoubtedly also.

Leadership is lost in intense turmoil and short-term crisis management, which is understandable.

This is "Apocalypse Now". Death must be avoided at all costs. They were in a butterfly flight and their wings have just been cut off. They are crashing.

The only perspective that their Leadership offers them is the Ostrich's Strategy: "We're going to deal with the shit for three years and try to survive until the clients come back and then, we'll start all over again just as before the pandemic.

In the meantime, no Future.

This is comparable to the caterpillar's system breakdown. No more jobs. Some People are put out of work or fired.

The others are supposed to stay and manage the crisis. Their only horizon is the "illusionary hope" that one day, in a future three years from now, the Future will be back, just as "before".

What can you imagine people in this company are experiencing?

What is the story they tell themselves?

Can the story of "the Future that will be more of the same later" convince them?

Is it a story that makes sense when COVID -19 has only accelerated the global awareness that things can no longer go back to "Business as Usual"?

We think that these people are confronted with the "Nostalgia of the Future": the Future like a long, quiet river which they dreamt about will never return. Deep down, they probably know it.

This is precisely the time to implement Shapership™, the "Art of shaping the Future", and the type of Butterfly Thinking that lies at its core.

These people need a different Horizon, they need to create an alternative story of the Future, not to bury their head in the sand, nor to create new illusions.

But precisely to re-establish their own Agency, to become actors and authors of their Destiny. They need to Re-Story their Future with a meaningful and Transformative Vision which opens a new lens, full of Hope and desires. And then make it happen.

Butterfly Thinking can create awareness of the Present, the Future and the Transition at the same time; moreover, it allows to move from Panic to Creation.

The Shapership™ attitude means having a true conversation about the situation, like the Shapers do, i.e.

1. See the situation "as it is": face the challenges of the declining, even crashing system, and instead of just "accusing" the outside circumstances, consciously examine how their taken-for-granted approach contributes to the fragility of the System and to the crash. That's a way to re-establish Responsibility: "Response Ability"

2. See the situation "as it could be": envision the Future and a completely new system, based on new Values, in tune with the NO MAD Land we cannot deny is emerging. What if we take this opportunity now, to put our imaginal cells at work to envision that Butterfly?

3. See how we can navigate the transition, considering the need to "redesign the plane whilst flying it". What can we make happen right now to avoid the disaster? How can we "improve" what needs to be maintained? What transformative action can we take to shift towards a viable Future? What cluster of imaginal cells can we assemble?

Here is an example of Shapership™ in action in a company

Imagine a CEO, busy with a fundamental question: "What's next for my company in this turbulent world?"

There are new issues to face. Shifts are happening outside!

His team and himself observe five ruptures in the Strategic Landscape

1. an Ecological rupture
2. a Digital rupture
3. an Economical rupture
4. an Organizational rupture
5. a Purpose rupture

He knows that, in order to make his company Future-Relevant, incremental approaches might be dangerous. Indeed, a game-changing world needs game-changing approaches.

It is not that his Strategy is not good. It is that the world in which this Strategy was working no longer exists!

THE ART OF SHAPERSHIP

The CEO knows all that. But that's easier said than done.

Why? Because that is a rational statement of what should be done.

But at the end and in a majority of cases, decisions are made for emotional reasons.

Moreover, we all know that

> *"Logic will never change emotions or perceptions"*. [119]

So, even IF his mental maps are regenerated and from now on, accurately represent the world as it is emerging, he might not be ready emotionally.

He might not be in the right state of Consciousness and of Being to find within himself the Courage to decide what *should* be decided and what the world calls for.

Instead of being radical, imaginative and purposeful, he might find himself trapped in the Regression Forces, tempted to preserve the status quo and the Comfort zone.

He might even fall into the illusion that short-term corrective measures or logical adjustments will be enough.

They certainly keep people busy.

But

> *"It is not because the ostrich buries her head in the sand that you can't kick her butt."*[120]

We once had to face such a case.

We knew the team was locked into a single story of their preferred Future: "Everything is fine". We make money."

---

[119] Edward de Bono, one of world's Highest authority in Serious Creativity

[120] Bernard Kouchner, French politician and physician. He is the co-founder of "Médecins sans Frontières" (MSF) and Médecins du Monde.

That story was so dominant that they could not see any alternative.

How could they make a wise decision about their Future, one that would engage thousands of people, based on such an assumption that "the Future will be the same as the Present"?

Rehearsing the Future

We co-created four scenario-based strategies which told four "stories" of alternative Futures for their company, depending on how much they could decide to be in tune with the world and operate from the Future. Those scenarios also made "visible" their taken for granted Beliefs and the way they were shaped by them.

Insert 13

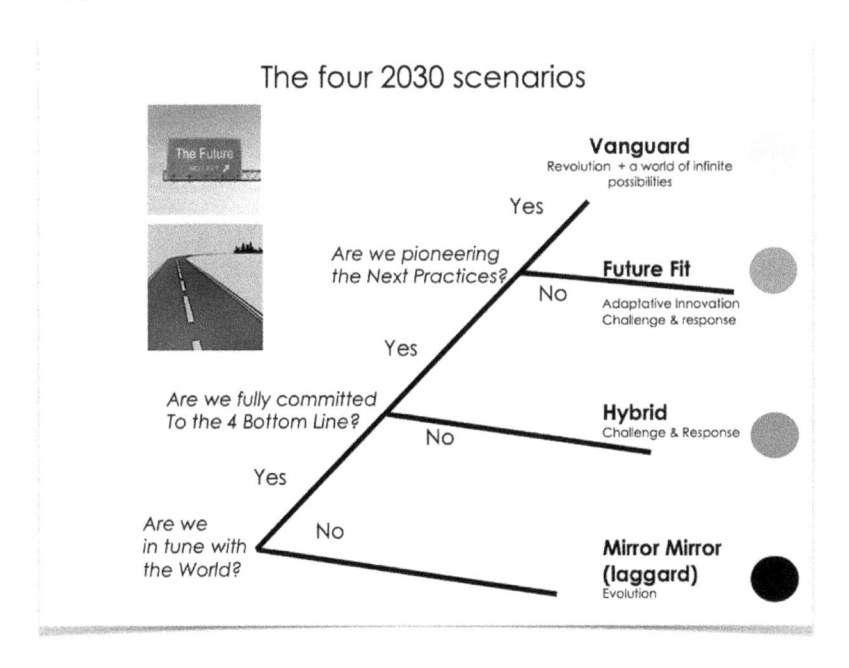

The four 2030 scenarios

Vanguard
Revolution + a world of infinite possibilities

Are we pioneering the Next Practices? — Yes

Future Fit
Adaptative Innovation
Challenge & response
— No

Are we fully committed To the 4 Bottom Line? — Yes

Hybrid
Challenge & Response
— No

Are we in tune with the World? — Yes

Mirror Mirror (laggard)
Evolution
— No

Scenarios one and two were ways to "Operate from the Past" and certainly not to operate as Shapers!

The first scenario – *Mirror Mirror* - was the story of minor adaptations, based on false assumptions that Business as Usual was enough to maintain Growth and that Change was optional.

The dominant model, assumptions and worldviews did not need to be challenged, nor even questioned: *"This is the way things are"*.

This scenario was mirroring the CEO's actual state of mind and beliefs.

It was also his "preferred Future", despite the fact that their current Business was not viable for the Future.

The tacit commitment on the "survival" of the system led to an implicit Strategy: "Play it safe with a minimum of risks and avoid any form of loss".

Nothing else could happen in that company unless he and his team accepted that they might be wrong (Very difficult for him!)

> *"The need to be right all the time is the biggest bar to new ideas"*[121]

The second scenario – *Hybrid* - was indeed a hybrid answer to the world and customer issues based on false assumptions about Customers and Innovation. Despite all the illusions they had, they started to operate in a financial bubble, but so disconnected from their customer's changing needs and demands that they could never bring them real "solutions".

The implicit strategy was "Limited Change, Survival through opportunities".

---

[121] Dr. Edward de Bono, Doctor in Psychology, Medicine and Philosophy. Author of more than 80 books and one of the world's highest Authority on Serious Creativity

What they called "Innovation" was likely to be drawn towards improving the status quo or, at its best, make things "better, cheaper, faster", but within the exact same unsustainable paradigm.

New source of Growth could not be found until they started looking at the question from an outside-in Customer perspective (how Customers experience their needs) versus an inside-out Business Perspective (how the company captures new sources of Growth).

Scenarios three and four were operating from the Future.

The third scenario – *Future Fit* - was based on the recognition that key issues of our time are wicked and demand complex transversal solutions.

It was based on the assumption that a full alignment with key issues of the world is not only indispensable in terms of Business. It gives Meaning to all actions.

An organic strategy could be chosen not to be a trend-setter but a fast follower to create multiple flows of competitive advantages and enable Growth while delivering purposeful outcomes.

The last scenario – *Vanguard* - emanated from a radically different attitude: the Altitude Attitude and an open Soul Compass.

It awakened the Shapers' enlarged and deeply humane Consciousness and the Desire to give new shapes to the world.

This scenario was a truly "alternative story", in tune with deeper trends and changes emerging in the Strategic landscape.

It was based on completely different assumptions, Values and worldviews, including what constitutes "Success", Excellence or "Value Creation".

And, most importantly, it was "aspirational" because it was woven with their hopes, dreams and desires to shift to a truly transformed viable Future rather than the implicit commitment to "fix" a failing system.

In this scenario, as Shapers would do, the CEO and his team would think big about themselves and about their contribution to Society. They would make their decisions based on consciously kept beliefs:

- If we want to be Future-relevant and useful, we need an enlarged and ECO-systemic perspective focused on the Life-sustaining solutions we can bring to real issues and the "transformational difference" we can make in people's lives

- Change is not optional, it is existential

- We need to make some serious strategic commitments which authentically resonate with the call we all feel for profound transformation towards another world, commitments that would encompass our Hopes, Faith, and Aspirations

- We need to act upon our commitments and have the courage to completely reinvent our approaches and shift from being inwardly to being outwardly focused, from eco-indifferent to eco-caring, from focused on Value Capture to focused on "Wealth Creation".

So, the daring implicit Strategy in this scenario was to make the metamorphosis from the caterpillar to the Butterfly: to purposefully disrupt the current "Business as Usual" and dare a complete turnaround to become a Future-Fit Organization, to pioneer the Next Best Practices, fully relevant to Society and to generate Inclusive Prosperity.

Once these four alternative Futures were built, they offered the team a reflective surface to make wiser choices and set priorities "now", with a sense of Hope and Purpose.

The entire team was able to reflect on their own Thinking and to see:

- That they were implicitly thinking and acting according to Mirror-Mirror, in their illusionary Comfort zone, completely dominated by a series of old worldviews and beliefs.
- that they definitely had to move to at least "Future Fit" …which remained a sort of rational way to outperform Competition
- That the scenario that they - at the same time - most desired and feared was the fourth: Vanguard
- That this "Vanguard" perspective, which was a radically different Future, got them out of a paradigm in which all Innovation is likely to be drawn towards improving the status quo or "disrupting it", but without fundamentally challenging their worldviews. Now they saw the space to design a longer-term portfolio of Innovation that would allow to transition from their current dominant pattern of activity to a completely different one
- That they could align what they SHOULD do with what they WANTED but that it required three shifts
    - ✓ a shift in INTENTION
    - ✓ a shift in FEELINGS
    - ✓ a shift in THINKING

For more details, see insert 12

Together,

1) They decided to creatively "resist" and challenge their own "dominant" ideas, worldviews, constructions, stories, "usual ways of operating" and to consciously

say a big NO to a system and its consequences which were no longer "fit-for-Purpose"

2) Since their imagination had been unlocked by the four stories of their "possible" Future, they could now clearly think Big about their contribution to the shaping of a new world. They said a Big Yes, with a full connection between Mind, Heart and Guts, to the Vanguard Scenario. Among the four possibilities, they chose the one that enhanced the Dignity, the Nobility and the Significance of Human Life. Not only because they "had" to, but most importantly, because they felt it was the "right" thing to do.

They now have a meaningful shared Meaning-Making Story of their Future. They behave like Shapers and collectively feel like Shapers

3) They are proudly busy on designing true "Anticipative Experimentations" to make it happen. They are "redesigning the plane whilst flying it" with a complete portfolio of Innovation consisting in three kind of actions: [122]

- Sustaining Innovations required to address concerns about the existing system in order to keep it running (e.g. Efficiency savings)
- Transformative Innovation that will pave the way for their Vision and Aspirations
- Aspects of the existing system that have no place in their imagined ideal Future and therefore need to be gradually "decommissioned"

This is how Shapership™ can inspire any individual, group or team to think and act with the Altitude Attitude and open alternative paths towards the Future that will not only enhance the Dignity and the Beauty of their Lives, but of everyone's Life.

---

[122] Inspired by our education and practice of the three Horizons framework at the International Futures Forum

Conclusions

To shape or not?
To shape, that is the question!

> *We have tried everything possible and none of it has worked. Now we must try the impossible.* Sun Ra

Humanity may still want to survive, but that will not be enough. Because we are beings of desires and we can't be satisfied by merely surviving in this world.

> "Half crushed under the weight of the progress it (Humanity) has made, it doesn't know enough that its future depends on itself. It's up to Humanity to see if it wants to go on living. It is then up to it to ask itself if it wants to live only, or to make the necessary effort so that the essential function of the universe, which is a machine for making gods, is accomplished on our refractory planet."[123]

We need to make this effort to "open the possibility of new possibilities", to transcend this Eternal Present and give

---
[123] Bergson, the two sources of morality and religion

ourselves a new Direction, an improbable but desirable Future that is in direct contact with our aspiration to live.

Acting as "gods" and "goddesses" might mean to insufflate the world with our Imagination, with a new Spirit, a new breadth to open a new horizon and build a new "Art of Living" that will at the same time support the Fabric of Life and enhance our Dignity.

We might develop a fertile thought capable of surpassing the Known, the Eternal Present, the already there. A thought that admits that the desire of the Future can be a "Cause" and that Imagination is another way to know the world. Especially the Unknown One.

As ways of Resisting to all the Regression Forces, we can practice Thinking, Dreaming, Imagining, Creating Infinite Possibilities, probable and improbable bifurcations, even miraculous ones.

We can put our Imagination at the service of the incalculable and stop the incalculable to be put at the service of calculation.

Vision creates Reality.

> ***"Those who do not believe in the impossible are kindly requested not to discourage those who are busy making it happen".*** Anonymous.

Instead of resenting the imaginal cells as enemies, we can join them and design new "communities of concern", within ourselves and outside

They are everywhere, some fully awaken, some like dormant "Shapers of the Future".

Their tiny voice may become a broad new choir.

Many big Nos and big YESSES can emerge to enable us to collectively give birth to a world with more space to be and to grow for all.

Thanks to the new "relationships" we create and shared Vision of the Future, we can better prepare to cross the threshold from the tamed territories of the "Known" to the untamed territories of a "new Imaginary".

> ***"Be careful about the Present you create because it must look like the Future you dream of".***
> Proverb from a Collective of Women in Bolivia.

Since "The eye only sees what the brain is ready to understand", we are called to open our eyes / minds to develop new types of Visions. Especially those eyes which are able to see that this world, which is in some way already upside down, needs to be turned upside down again.

Considering the issues we face, being careful today might be the opposite of Incremental Thinking. We are called to Radical Thinking, with an open Soul Compass, so we can combine the Courage and Lucidity to face a world we don't want anymore, with the Imagination needed to have daring Visions of a world we want more of.

We can consciously choose the "Erotica of the Future" and become "I Openers", "Eye Hopeners" and "High Hopeners".

Let us be true to ourself and useful to the journey!

About the Authors

Aline Frankfort

Aline is a Provocative Thinker + Artist (Photography and painting) + Narrative therapist + Consultant + Author + Professor + Fellow of the Louvain School of Management (university of Louvain-La-Neuve) + Woman in spiritual quest + Full Member of the Club of Rome, working for a better world.

She lives between Utopia and Reality, between the Impossible and the Possible.

Obsessed by her quest to understand "What is Reality?", she has sharpened her skills in "opening the doors of perceptions" to refresh and broaden our vision of the world as well as to enhance our capacities to craft meaning-making realities.

As a child, she kept drawing all the time and experienced in her flesh what Gaston Bachelard said: "Imagination awakens new Life and opens eyes that have new types of Vision".

Being dyslexic, she had a problem with repetitive and "linear" logic, and she developed the joyful practice of approaching things "upside down" and "downside up".

As an example, she always believed we had to reverse the traditional way of looking at things, attributed to Saint Thomas: "I only believe what I see". "I see what I believe" is much more appropriate. Hence the Title of this book "The eye only sees what the brain is ready to understand". (Bergson).

In the same vein, her quest is to make the Future we imagine the cause of the Present.

Her passion and profession are to help people develop the power and freedom to purposefully change the stories that shape their lives, so they can explore uncharted territories with imagination and shape desirable new realities.

She holds a law degree, 4 Executive Certificates from the M.I.T Sloan School of Management but above all, she is deeply influenced by her training with Edward de Bono, Master in Serious Creativity and Lateral Thinking as well as by her Narrative Practices and her encounter with her partner, Jean-Louis Baudoin.

Jean-Louis Baudoin

Jean-Louis is a Life Raiser and Fun Raiser + Promoter of Serious Creativity + Jazz double bassist & percussionist + award-winning copywriter (Saatchi & Saatchi) + Exceptional concepts and name-finder + Creative Thinker + Consultant + Coach in Persuasive Presentation skills +Author + Professor/ Lecturer

Jean-Louis embodies Serious Creativity. He loves opening new Perceptions and Possibilities, convinced that they can lead us to realize a concrete Utopia: new attitudes, new relations, new behaviors.

For him Brotherhood and Sisterhood are just around our cortex!

He helps people boost their creative Mindsets and Skillsets to live a life richer in possibilities and meaning.

Among his passions: attentively provoking movement and helping people to get out of their limits, see things with Altitude and lightness, open doors to the future, developing creative concepts and names. By the way, he is the inventor of the Concept of Shapership™.

His other passion: he is a confirmed Jazz Musician (double bass), and has played with people like Toots Thielemans, Nathalie Loriers, Jean-François Prins, Eric Legnini and Félix Simtaine. Using his talents and the Jazz Combo Metaphor, he conveys the Art of Collaboration in a workshop.

He embodies an original, diversified and creative life and is recognized for his openness, humor, creative genious, fantastic Storytelling abilities and sense of Harmony - he has been "diagnosed" in a Thesis written at the University of Illinois as "***the Third man***", capable of building bridges between cultures.

After early exposure to foreign Cultures at age 17 (South Africa as Rotary Fellow and The United States the same year as American Field Service Exchange Student), he obtains a Doctorate in Law from Liège University and has then reinvented himself seven times:

- Manager of an international student travel program designed to enable Culture exchanges

- Award-winning copywriter (Saatchi & Saatchi, Festival de Cannes)
- Exceptional concepts and name-finder
- Inventor of "In-Store'", a second-hand Contemporary high-class Design store
- «Toqued» restaurant owner
- Expert audiovisual scenario writer
- Coach in persuasive Presentation Skills and Negotiation

Jean-Louis has joined forces with Aline in 1992.

The Team

We consider ourselves Mind-openers or Eye Hopeners.

Both invited professors in Creative Thinking and Strategic Innovation, we have more than 20 years of experience with leading companies, research centers and entrepreneurs.

The Art of shaping the Future is our passion.

We have blended together Wisdom, Humour, Academia, Neuroscience, Creative lenses, Jazz, extensive Know Hows, Unorthodox approaches and Passion to generate "Shifts in Minds for Shifts in Action".

We are committed to support people, teams and communities to make Transformative journeys into the Future with a soul compass.

We help them face their challenges and explore the Future with the **Imagination, Radical Thinking, Unconventional Wisdom and Creativity** needed to escape the repetition of the S.O.S. (i.e. Same old Solutions, the polite version of Same Old Shit) and **shape a radically different and desirable Future.**

This opens acres of new mental and concrete territories for Innovation and helps them to build the Future on **Lucidity** as well as on **Transformative Visions.**

Our Passion for intentional Change(s) led us to write our first book "Shapership™, the Art of Shaping the Future" (published in 2018 in French), followed by the creation of a series of Practices to put it into concrete action.

We spread this concept through consultancy, using a "Strategic Futuring" approach; our Shapership™ Academi (with an I for Imagination), an original educational project dedicated to learning the Mindsets and Skillsets needed to shape the Future; the production and dissemination of knowledge, through books, **articles, and modules taught at top universities.**

Shapership™ stands for building the Future on Imagination, Desire, Hope and Radical Wisdom, to resist Stupidity, Fear, Despair and Violence.

Annex

Discover more On shapership™

Shapership™ is a concept designed to open new windows in our mind. Based on **"Shifts in Minds for Shifts in Action"**, it helps us redraw our mental maps and get to place we haven't imagined before.

Created by Aline Frankfort and Jean-Louis Baudoin, Shapership™ makes radically different futures visible and desirable.

Discover the **concept**, our **book** as well as the **practices** we use to spread Shapership™: Strategic Futuring (Consultancy), events and formats like our Shapership™ Academi, the production and dissemination of knowledge, through books, articles, and modules teach at top universities.

https://www.shapership.com/

On MAD Land and NO-MAD Land

https://www.shapership.com/our-services/from-roadmapping-to-broadmapping

Blog articles

https://www.shapership.com/blog/the-next-wise-move-from-mad-land-to-no-mad-land

https://www.shapership.com/blog/wise-moves-from-mad-land-to-no-mad-land-5

https://www.shapership.com/blog/wise-moves-from-mad-land-to-no-mad-land-2

https://www.shapership.com/blog/from-realism-blind-spot-to-potentiality-spring-board

https://www.shapership.com/blog/broadmapping

On Jazz and Collaboration

https://www.shapership.com/our-services/jazz-and-collaboration

https://www.shapership.com/blog/jamming-together-a-new-art-of-collaboration-in-vuca-times

Listen to Jean-Louis's podcast

https://www.shapership.com/episode/jazz-and-the-art-of-collaboration

Ingram Content Group UK Ltd.
Milton Keynes UK
UKHW020845190423
420422UK00014B/625